DDGP

Fraternally Yours

Identify Fraternal Groups and Their Emblems

Peter Swift Seibert

Schiffer Publishing Ltd
4880 Lower Valley Road, Atglen, Pennsylvania 19310

Schiffer Books are available at special discounts for bulk purchases for sales promotions or premiums. Special editions, including personalized covers, corporate imprints, and excerpts can be created in large quantities for special needs. For more information contact the publisher:

Schiffer Publishing Ltd.
4880 Lower Valley Road
Atglen, PA 19310
Phone: (610) 593-1777; Fax: (610) 593-2002
E-mail: Info@schifferbooks.com

For the largest selection of fine reference books on this and related subjects, please visit our website at **www.schifferbooks.com**
We are always looking for people to write books on new and related subjects. If you have an idea for a book, please contact us at proposals@schifferbooks.com

This book may be purchased from the publisher. Include $5.00 for shipping. Please try your bookstore first. You may write for a free catalog.

In Europe, Schiffer books are distributed by
Bushwood Books
6 Marksbury Ave.
Kew Gardens
Surrey TW9 4JF England
Phone: 44 (0) 20 8392 8585; Fax: 44 (0) 20 8392 9876
E-mail: info@bushwoodbooks.co.uk
Website: www.bushwoodbooks.co.uk

All text by author
Photos by Ken Munro
Library of Congress Control Number: 2012930640

Designed by Stephanie Daugherty
Type set in Slimbach Medium/Zurich BT
ISBN: 978-0-7643-4060-4
Printed in China

Contents

Acknowledgments & Dedication

It has been said that "America is a nation of joiners." For 200 years, my family has provided ample proof of this statement. From Woodmen to the Royal Arcanum to the temperance halls of the The Woman's Christian Temperance Union (WCTU), we have joined dozens of groups. Nowhere, however, does this history come through more strongly or extend as deeply as to when it comes to Freemasonry. For more than 150 years and through five generations, the men in my family have been Freemasons. Just before my beloved grandfather died, he pulled me aside as a 12

year old to ask that I follow in his footsteps and join a lodge. At the age of 21, I followed through on that promise.

Fraternally Yours is dedicated to my Masonic relations. This includes my father, Norman E. Seibert, my grandfather, Harley L. Swift, my great grandfather, William H. Barr, and my great-great grandfather, Hugh D. Barr. I also want to thank my great uncle Albert L. Swift, who taught my grandfather, and through him to me, the importance of the lessons of the Craft. To all of these men, I am proud to call you my Brothers.

Special thanks is given to my father-in-law and noted author, Ken Munro of Lancaster County. Despite his own busy writing schedule, coupled with helping to take care of his granddaughter and my daughter, Mary, he found time to beautifully photograph all the images for this book. Thanks Ken for your great work!

Finally, many thanks to my wife, Kim Seibert, for her efforts to coordinate my words, photographs, and captions. This would never have happened without ya!

I

Explaining Fraternal Societies

Anyone who is not familiar with the nature of how fraternal organizations function will quickly be overwhelmed by the complex, and sometimes contradictory, terminology that they use. Thus it is important to begin with some brief definitions and explanations. I should note that for the purposes of this book, a fraternal organization is defined as one that holds meetings, elects officers, has a distinctive ritual, and wears a unique badge. I have focused primarily upon the major late 19th and early 20th century organizations and almost exclusively upon those found in the United States. This book is neither an encyclopedia nor a history of American fraternalism. Rather it is intended to give the layman a look at the different types of regalia worn by fraternal societies.

By their very nature, fraternal groups have a functional and organized structure. They meet as a body, often in a lodge or hall. A lodge or hall is simply a location designated for holding meetings. Usually, such halls have formal meeting rooms, a dining room, and accompanying kitchen, and often a card or recreational room. In the 19th and early 20th centuries, such halls were usually two- or three-story buildings located in the heart of a downtown. The first floor would be leased to a commercial tenant to help pay the expenses of the rest of the building. The second floor, heavily curtained, was the ceremonial meeting room strategically situated there to prevent curious eyes from viewing the secret ceremonies. The upper floors were reserved for social rooms, kitchens, smoking lounges, and card rooms. Today, the aging population of fraternal groups has meant a shift towards more suburban locations with ground level buildings that have lots of parking.

Most fraternal groups organize themselves around an elected presiding officer and two vice presidents. In addition, there is an elected secretary and/or treasurer who are often chosen from the ranks of past presidents. The presiding officer then appoints various other officers to perform the rituals of the organization. There is a general line of succession among the appointed and elected officers with each person serving in turn as they move up the line. Generally, the bottom position is the outer guard who closes and locks the outside door of the meeting room while the group is in session. There is often an inner door guard and several officers charged with carrying messages, moving candidates through rituals, and helping to open or close a meeting. Finally a chaplain is present to provide prayers at appropriate moments. The titles may change for these positions but fundamentally their tasks remain the same for each group.

Regalia is a wonderful term that is applied to the myriad of medals, ribbons, aprons, sashes, collars, and costumes that are worn by members of fraternal groups. Generally, one can lump regalia into two categories: ceremonial items only worn in a closed

This collection of six coin silver lodge jewels was made in Philadelphia probably circa 1850. Sadly, the identity of the organization is not known. They appear to be a set of officer's jewels with the various badges of the office centered within the circle. The dove is usually the symbol of a messenger while the swords are that of an inner or outer guard.

The flag could represent the flag bearer in the lodge. The triangle with other symbols perhaps represents one of the elected officers. They are marked on the back with the name of the engraver but no other identifying marks. Size: 4 ½"

Although beyond the scope of this book, there are a host of other quasi-fraternal organizations associated with high schools and colleges. Fraternities, sororities, honor societies, clubs, and others exist academically and mirror the national fascination with fraternalism of the adults. This is a small high school pennant to which the original owner has pinned numerous small pins and badges. Some are rewards of merit for outstanding work or member's badges in various honor societies. Size: ¾" to 1" in length

meeting usually for an initiation and those items that are worn in business meetings, as well as in public. For the purpose of this book, we are focusing upon the regalia worn in public or at business meetings rather than ceremonial just for initiation.

While it is always dangerous to generalize, it would be safe to say that nearly all fraternal societies copy, at some level, the regalia of the Masonic fraternity. As the oldest, and the most fashionable, of the fraternal societies, Freemasonry set a standard that other groups have continued to

Here is a case where the context needs to be understood in order to determine the use of a particular item. This heavy pair of coin silver crossbones is marked on the reverses: "Sanborn/Lowell Mass/Coin" for the maker. They have large loops for stitching applied to the back. This device was originally stitched to the front of a Masonic Knights Templar apron and represented mortality. The apron, probably dating from the Civil War period, has now disappeared and so all that survives are the silver bones.
Size: 6"

copy. Even among those groups that deliberately set out to be different, their regalia still closely relates to a Masonic type.

Masonic tradition calls for officers, and usually most members, to appear in specific regalia at meetings or for public ceremonial occasions such as funerals. This is an apron, sash, or collar that all members wear with the officers (past and present) having more elaborate trim and decoration on their examples. Additionally, almost all fraternal groups have a range of badges and medals that are worn for service within the organization or among the community at large. Those medals are worn on the chest much like military decorations.

Fraternal symbols can appear in the most obscure of places. This is an English horse brass with the square and compass located within the central rosette. It is likely that this was worn by a horse whose master was a Freemason. Probably dating from the last quarter of the nineteenth century. Size: 5"

First and foremost are "jewels" which is a Masonic term referring to a distinctive medal given for service as a past presiding officer of a local, regional, state or national body. Jewels can be made up of real jewels, cut glass brilliants, gold, silver, or plain gilded base metals. They are generally the most elaborate of personal regalia and many organizations require that upon the death of the recipient that they be returned to the issuing body.

Collars are usually either a metal or fabric collar (often with a chain across the middle to keep the collar situated in the middle of the wearer's back and chest) with a central pendent noting the rank of the individual. Collars are generally only worn on ceremonial occasions and in most cases must be returned upon the death of the owner. Commonly, speaking, collars are worn as emblems of past or present rank in an organization.

This hand-colored photograph dates from the 1880s and shows an officer in the lodge regalia of the Odd Fellows. The apron and matching sash were to be worn in lodges while the collar only on public occasions. The image was originally taken by a photographer and then hand colored in his studio to bring out details. Notice that the face was not touched and so appears more washed out than the rest of the image. It is indistinctly signed in the lower front and is housed in an original period faux marbled frame.
Size: 8"

Most fraternal organizations have medals or badges that are given for length of membership within the organization. These pins or medals are usually given for 25 or 50 years of service. In addition, groups also will give medals for service in the military and particularly in time of war.

A final distinction is between honors and awards presented by an organization. Generally speaking, an award is actively sought and earned by the recipient. This can include the youth group awards for outstanding scholarship. Honors are nominated, often in secret, by others and given for general service to the organization or humanity in general.

One of the most puzzling aspects of fraternal regalia is the variation in size, style, and quality of work even within a given jurisdiction. It makes collecting and identifying fraternal regalia a challenge. For example, a Masonic Past Master's jewel from Nebraska is a small gold medal, while that from Pennsylvania is a large and glitzy silver square replete with bars and clasps. Both jewels are for service as a past presiding officer of a Masonic lodge and yet they are visually as different as night and day. Variations even within lodges also exist. A rich lodge will often present an elaborate jewel while a less affluent one will opt for something similar – hence

OPPOSITE: This carte de visite depicts a young man wearing a wide range of seemingly dis-similar regalia and uniform elements. The hat is loosely patterned on the U.S. military Hardee hat (Model 1858) of the pre-Civil War era. The badge on his chest appears to be that of the Knights of Pythias although it is difficult to be sure. The elaborate sash with gold wire stars is the most striking. A badge in the center appears to have a dove in a circle which could identify the wearer as a member of the Odd Fellows. Unfortunately, like much fraternal regalia of the Civil War period, there are few good resources to turn to in identifying regalia. The image was photographed by Patton and Dietrich in Reading who worked from 1861 to 1869.
Size: 3" x 4"

the reason that many organizations have adopted rigid and hard rules about the style of regalia.

In collecting or studying the regalia of fraternal organizations, it is important to always be prepared to be surprised by some variation or change. No one is a complete expert on the subject and there is vastly more bad information out there than good and reliable material.

Balloting upon new members is one of the most serious and solemn tasks in any fraternal organization. Each group has its own rules and regulations about how many white balls will elect someone and how many will reject. The process is anonymous and conducted within strict rules. This ballot box dates from circa 1910 and is made of oak. Note that the handle is at the opposite end of the balloting section in order to prevent anyone from seeing or tampering with the ballots. Size: 14" x 9"

A whole subset of collecting fraternal regalia can be built around the personalized shaving mugs that were a feature of barber shops a hundred years ago. This example bearing a square and compass is among the most common to have been produced. Nearly all the other fraternal societies illustrated in this book utilized similar mugs. Size: 5"

Another area beyond the scope of this book but with ceremonies, titles, and forms of recognition similar to fraternal societies are trade unions. This small badge was given for 25 years of service to "F. Rickman" by the Brotherhood of Railway Carman of America. Made of 10 karet gold, the badge has a large stamp on the reverse as well showing that it was union made.
Size: 1 ½"

The Good Templars was a fraternal and benefit society that existed in England and the United States during the late 19th century. This small English souvenir medal was made to commemorate the visit of the English Grand Officers to St. George's Hall in Liverpool in the late 1880s.
Size: 3"

Even in small towns such as Huron, South Dakota, there was interest and pride in being a member of the Odd Fellows. This father, son, and possibly grandson are all wearing the sashes and collar of Odd Fellowship. In communities such as Huron, fraternal lodges (regardless of what organization) played an important social role in communities. They also served to bind families together as in the case of these generations of Odd Fellowship.
Size: 8" x 7"

The importance of belonging to a fraternal society is best typified by this late 19th century image of a gentleman with a Masonic stick pin in his cravat. The pin is the single object that the viewer is immediately drawn to, whether in the image or real life. His membership in his lodge was something important to this unknown gentleman.
Size: 5" x 7"

II

Freemasonry

The impact of Freemasonry on American society from the Colonial period to the present is a fascinating subject for study. Whether in rural, urban, or suburban areas of the country, Masonic lodges have flourished. Through fun groups like the Shriners or Tall Cedars, vast amounts of money have been funneled to charitable and philanthropic interests. Freemasons have come from every walk of life from Presidents to day laborers. Generations (five in my case) have been members of lodges. Even pop culture, particularly through the writings of Dan Brown and Catherine Kurtz and in films such as *National Treasure*, have made the name into a household word.

The specific moment of creation for Freemasonry is unknown, but by and large scholars today place it at a point in the late 1580s. Freemasonry was a product of a number of English intellectual movements coming at the end of the Renaissance. One theory is that stone or operative masons began to accept outsiders, particularly intellectuals, who saw the precepts of architecture as moral lessons. Thus, a man should be square with someone, always true, and on the level.

This is a traveling certificate issued by the Grand Lodge of New South Wales to a constituent member. Most Grand Lodges around the word issue such documents to allow their members to visit other jurisdictions. The situation becomes more complex, however, insofar as not every Grand Lodge recognizes every other one. As a result, members when traveling have to be cautious in determining if their Grand Lodge is on friendly terms with the one they are visiting. Written in English and Latin on vellum and dated 1953. Size: 24" x 18"

This wonderfully mustached man is shown wearing the collar, apron, and gauntlets of a Worshipful Master of his lodge under the Grand Lodge of England. American lodges do not generally wear the decorative cuffs or gauntlets as their English counterparts did. Marked "H & R Stiles./8, Kensington High, St W."
Size: 5" x 7"

These builders' terms conveying a new dual meaning. The earliest lodges met in taverns and combined meetings with a convivial evening replete with toasts. Single lodges soon began to join together as district and ultimately national "Grand Lodges." Variations in ritual evolved and there was an abundance of additional degrees available for an extra initiation fee or to commemorate service.

Spreading from England to the rest of the United Kingdom and from there throughout the balance of the British Empire, Freemasonry was introduced into the American colonies at a relatively early point. Because there were was no single "Grand Lodge" for all Freemasons, numerous jurisdictions (Scotland, Ireland, and two in England) claimed the right to start subordinate lodges in colonial America leading to a veritable crazy quilt of different bodies and practices. From this, grew the present American system of fifty different jurisdictions of Freemasons in the United States. Even in America where bigger is almost always seen to be better, the idea of fifty different sovereign Grand Lodges with fifty different Grand Masters seems very complex and strange. Yet because each state's grand lodge was begun by a different chartering body, there is no uniform Grand Master for all of the United States. Each state is sovereign issuing its own regalia and laying claim to all members within its borders. Thus, a Pennsylvania Freemason cannot concurrently join a lodge in another state without first giving up his Pennsylvania affiliation.

Lodge membership grew in the United States rapidly. By the early 19th century, most publicly elected officials were members. This ultimately resulted in a public backlash based upon a fear that

The Pennsylvania Masonic Past Master's regalia is one of the most distinctive in the United States. The Ahiman Rezon or Book of Decisions lays out very specific rules as to the shape, size, and quality of a Past Master's jewel. Made of silver (gold being reserved for Past Grand officers), the Past Master's jewel has changed remarkably little over the last 100 years. Most are made in Philadelphia with the author having seen at least one by the noted firm of Bailey, Banks, and Biddle. The jewel incorporates small tools on the arms of the square with the Past Master's lodge number appearing on the small apron in the middle. The jewel is hung with three silver bars. The top being a pattern suspension bar, the middle with the year the individual served as Master of the lodge and the bottom with his initials. The reverse has the name, lodge name, and year of service engraved on it. It should be noted that Pennsylvania lodge jewels are considered the property of the lodge and thus are to be returned upon the death of the Past Master. Many lodges, in order to save money, will then re-engrave and re-issue the jewel. This example was presented to Isaac Wilbur Heisey by Brownstone Lodge No. 666 in Hershey, Pennsylvania, for service in 1971.
Size: 6"

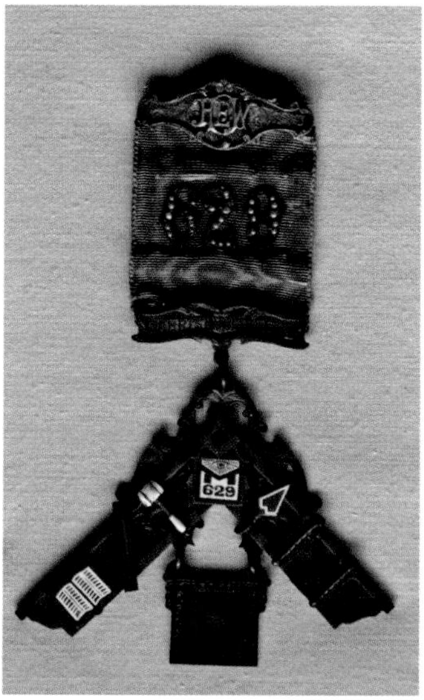

This Pennsylvania Past Master's jewel shows a variation in style from the preceding example. Here the lodge number is applied as individual numbers to the center of the ribbon. This was presented to Henry G. Warner, Past Master of Harrisburg, Pennsylvania Lodge 629 in 1918.
Size: 6"

Each state has its own distinctive Past Master's Jewel. Many jurisdictions opt for small, detailed medals to be worn on the pocket of a jacket or even a lapel. This example is of the square, compass and all-seeing eye of God. Made in 10 karat gold, it was presented to Ira C. Lehr, Past Master of George Washington Lodge in Lincoln, Nebraska, in 1955.
Size: 2 ½"

The Grand Lodge of Pennsylvania has never favored issuing medals for service, instead preferring to give pins. Shown here is a very rare World War One service pin given to "Samuel K. Fawcett/1931." The pin is sterling silver with enamels on the front. A minor mystery is the number "21"on the tail of the buckle around the border.
Size: 1"

At their peak of membership, many of the Grand Lodges began producing large quantities of medals and badges for their members in commemoration of any number of activities and events. This fine badge, made by the Whitehead and Hoag Company, was produced for visitors attending the sessions of the Grand Lodge of Michigan in 1911.
Size: 4"

One custom that seems common to most American lodges is to award a medal or pin for long membership, usually of fifty years. Since membership in a lodge is restricted to those 21 years old or older, such fifty-year pins or medals are highly prized. This example was awarded by the Grand Lodge of Massachusetts to George Kellstrand and is dated 1944. It is also interesting to note the Veteran bar on the top. If Kellstrand joined his lodge at age 21 in 1894, then it is likely his military veteran service was for the Spanish-American War.
Size: 5"

the centering of power within a secret society would lead to corruption. Out of this was the founding of the short-lived Anti-Masonic Party of the 1830s. This one-issue party focused its energies on eliminating Freemasonry from Americana society. Today, it is remembered as America's first populist third political party. Like all one-issue parties, the energy needed to sustain it soon waned, and by the time of the Civil War, antimasonry as a political movement was dead. By the late 1860s, Freemasonry had rebounded and grew rapidly during the remainder of the century. Freemasonry has gone through an endless number of peaks and valleys in its history. Interestingly, even at its lowest points, it has been able to retain a substantial community visibility marking it as the most successful of all fraternal groups.

This pair of images shows the interior of a simple Masonic lodge hall thought to be in the Midwestern United States. The room is simply furnished as the image shows. There is Victorian strip carpeting set on the floor which would have given the room a richness of appearance and also deadened the sound of walking. These two photographs show the room looking east (towards the Master's pedestal) and west (towards that of the Senior Warden). Note the columns flanking those stations as well as the three tapers set to the side of the altar on the floor of the lodge. The oak chairs and furnishings were mass produced for lodge use such as this. Circa 1890-1900.
Size: 4" x 5"

This photograph shows a Scottish lodge member wearing the apron of his lodge and a parade sash. American lodges never wore such sashes preferring a more restrained appearance when in public. Marked Hamton/Glasgow.
Size: 5" x 7"

All men must petition and then join the basic Blue or Symbolic Lodge where they receive three ritualistic degrees that qualify them to be known as Freemasons. The Blue Lodge is presided over by an elected Master and two wardens and is served by about a half dozen appointed ceremonial officers along with an elected treasurer and secretary. Succession to office in a lodge generally begins with appointment to the first "chair" and continues through election as Junior Warden, Senior Warden, and Worshipful Master. From there, an ambitious Past Master can seek appointment as a District Deputy Grand Master or ultimately to be elected to serve as Grand Master of his respective jurisdiction.

Masonic regalia harkens back to the clothing of the builder's trades. Thus all members wear aprons that

Outside of service as a Past Master, lodges are limited in what other jewels they can award to former officers. Service as the lodge Secretary or Treasurer is the one exception. This rather shiny jewel was awarded to a long serving secretary of a lodge. Interestingly, the owner was also a Past Master and since Masonic decorum prohibits wearing multiple jewels, it is unlikely that this Past Secretary's jewel was worn much. Engraved "T. F. Sallade P.M./ Williamson No. 307/1973-1983."
Size: 6 ½"

This small badge was awarded by the Grand Lodge of Ohio to members and guests attend the 1918 meeting or communication of the state body. The badge is marked on the reverse "F.M. Noble and Company."
Size: 3"

This fifty-year medal for service as a lodge member was presented by the Grand Lodge of New York to Brother Carl Mayer who was made a Master Mason on November 5, 1896. The medal is marked on the edge by the "Medallic Art Company/bronze" who made many such lodge medals over the years.
Size: 5"

The Grand Lodge of England operates several facilities for elderly members, boys, and girls. Those who give money to support those organizations are named as Stewards and receive the illustrated badge to wear during that year. Many American lodge members send gifts to these benevolent organizations in order to receive and wear such badges. Marked Glendenning and Son/London.

This medal, probably because of its weight not being intended to be worn, was given as a souvenir of the 1983 Masonic Congress in Costa Rica. While each Grand Lodge is separate and sovereign, regular meetings are held worldwide by the various grand bodies in order to discuss issues of common interest. Size: 2"

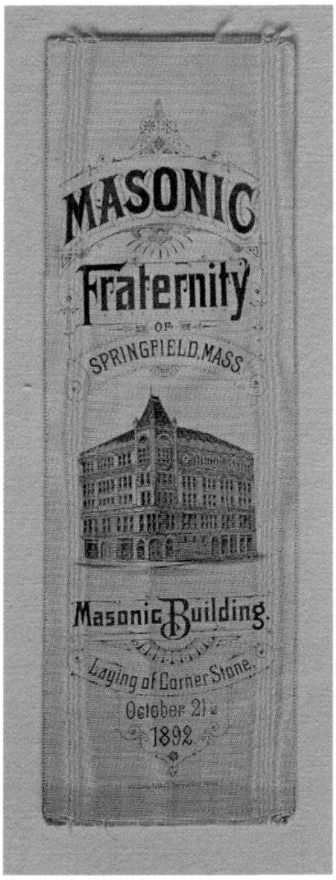

The opening of a new Masonic temple, compete with elaborate ceremonies by the local or grand lodge, was an important event in many local communities. These silk ribbons were produced and given to lodge members attending those ceremonies.
Size: 5" x 1 ½"

Masonic lodge founding anniversary banquets are a unique sub-group within the larger sphere of Masonic commemoratives. Lodges celebrated their anniversary of founding by hosting a large dinner with unique ceremonies (known as a table lodge) and a speaker. In commemoration of that night, they often issued special mugs, glasses or silver napkin rings. This is an English sterling silver example dating from the early 20th century.
Size: 3"

are loosely derived from the work aprons of operative masons. Similarly, the tools of the building trade (square, compass, plumb, level) figure on the regalia in infinite variations. As a universal organization, overt religious symbols are not permitted on lodge regalia although occasionally Old Testament references to the building of King Solomon's temple can be found.

There are two sidebar issues that need to be addressed as it relates to Masonic regalia. First is that all Freemasons must belong to a Blue or Symbolic lodge in order to be considered a Freemason. Beginning in the 18th century and continuing to the present, there have been Freemasons who sought higher or more advanced knowledge beyond that which was communicated in the rituals of the Blue lodge. As a result, they created and/or joined dozens of other organizations including the Scottish Rite and York Rite. They also founded groups based solely on fellowship and conviviality such as the Shrine,

This is the large presentation table medal given by Pennsylvania Grand Master John L. McCain (dated 1976) to local Worshipful Master's and other dignitaries. A small coin-size medal was available for purchase. Pennsylvania Grand Masters, as well as those from other jurisdictions, had these unique and distinctive table medals produced for presentation as gifts. Marked on the edge "Medallic Art Company."
Size: 4"

This novelty piece cast in aluminum was produced for the Belly Masons/6:30 degree. This unofficial group gathered prior to lodge meetings. If a member neglected to bring this token, then he had to pay for the meals for all the others in attendance.
Size: 1 ½"

This is the small, coin-size medallion of the larger John L. McCain. This could be purchased by any member.
Size: 2"

Grotto, and Tall Cedars of Lebanon. They developed organizations for women (Eastern Star, White Shrine, Amaranth) and for their sons (DeMolay) and daughters (Rainbow and Job's Daughters). Each of these groups has their own regalia and ritual. However, and this is vital to understand, none of these groups are superior in any way to the Blue or Symbolic Lodge. A man

Individual lodges also produced commemorative pocket medals that were given during their anniversary banquets. Most are cast with various Masonic imagery (square, compass, trowel) as well as the name of the lodge and its anniversary date. This example is Milton, Pennsylvania, and is dated 1976.
Size: 1"

This commemorative pocket medal or coin was produced by Sunbury Lodge No. 22 for its 200th anniversary in 1979.
Size: 2"

who joins all the other groups but neglects to keep his membership in his basic lodge will automatically be expelled from those other groups.

Second is that beginning in the 18th century and continuing, albeit with some limited inroads, down to the present, Freemasonry in the United States has been racially divided. As a result, there are a series of parallel

Another commemorative item frequently made by lodges to give as anniversary or other gifts are miniature trowels. This example was given by the Worshipful Master of Lodge 22 to the Past Masters. Size: 5"

Masonic bodies for black men that are identical to those for whites. This is an unfortunate system clouded by the fact that the white Grand Lodges have, until recently, refused recognition of black lodges within their own state. This has begun to change in some jurisdictions but much work needs to be done in this area. Black Masonic lodges, known as Prince Hall Masonry (named for a former slave who is believed to have founded the American black lodge system) have similar regalia although with some variances. Examples will be shown in the chapter under Prince Hall Masonry.

This 50-year jewel was issued by the Grand Lodge of Maine to Barker L. Burbank. Size: 5"

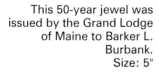

III

Royal Arch and Mark Masonry

The best current research suggests that the Royal Arch degree of Freemasonry is of some antiquity and was created as an extension of the third or Master Mason's degree. It, along with the degree of Past Master, Most Excellent Master, and Mark Mason constitute, in the United States, the degrees conferred in a Royal Arch Chapter. Next to the Scottish Rite, the Royal Arch is perhaps the most popular Masonic body for a Mason to join outside of his own lodge.

Membership in the Royal Arch historically required service as a Past Master (former presiding officer) of a

This is a most unusual piece whose origins and use are not clear. It was acquired without provenance from a dealer in Kentucky and probably is from a back-country Royal Arch Chapter. This is mostly likely the center pendant jewel from a High Priest's collar. It is made of cut brass with hand engraved Blue Lodge and Royal Arch emblems. Interestingly, the central triangle features a man with a top hat and cane that is engraved on both the obverse and reverse (while the remainder of the engraving on the hollow triangle is only on the front). Size: 5"

It is difficult to distinguish between American and English Royal Arch member jewels. This example is probably American and commemorates the membership of Maurice Rainey in 1932. Distinguishing elements include the keystone, enamel oval with the initials KSHTWSST, and the phrase "Holiness to the Lord."
Size: 3″

This is a Pennsylvania-style Past High Priest's jewel. Unlike other jurisdictions that use brilliants in their jewels, the Pennsylvania examples are very restrained. This example includes three top bars showing the chapter "Northumberland," the letters "PHP" for Past High Priest, and the chapter number on the registry of Pennsylvania chapters "174." The reverse is engraved "Presented to Edward H. Walker/ by Northumberland RAC #174/ December 27, 1969."
Size: 5"

This is an American Royal Arch apron. Much simpler than the Scottish example shown here, this is typical of what most American Royal Arch masons would wear. It is of lambskin with a silk ribbon and simple ties. Probably mid-western and circa 1920.
Size: 30"

This apron and accompanying sash are part of the regalia worn by a Scottish Royal Arch Mason. The apron is of lambskin with a satin red and blue sawtooth border. The matching sash is of the same material. Each grand chapter, like the grand lodges, has regalia that is distinctive from its neighbors. In the United States, members would not be permitted to wear such elaborate aprons. Such work would be reserved for elected and past officers. Circa 1950.
Size: 29"

Blue lodge. However, as this would severely limit the ability of Royal Arch chapters to grow, it was commonly agreed in most jurisdictions to virtually confer the title, but not the rank, of a Past Master. This rule holds true in every jurisdiction except Pennsylvania where the Blue Lodge exclusively holds the degree of Past Master. As a result, it cannot be conferred in a Royal Arch Chapter. Thus, in Pennsylvania, members of the Royal Arch are not Past Masters.

Another degree conferred in a Royal Arch chapter is the Mark Master Mason's degree. This degree has not always been under the control of Royal Arch Chapters and in some jurisdictions is actually conferred in its own body—a Mark Lodge. Part of the Mark degree is the adoption by the candidate of a distinctive sign or mark by the member. It is the custom then to have that emblem then engraved on a small token or pocket

This is a traveling certificate for a Royal Arch Mason allowing him to visit other chapters. It is an interesting document for several reasons. First in that the Grand Royal Arch Chapter of Scotland is the issuing body although the recipient is from New South Wales. Because Freemasonry, particularly within the British Empire, spread unevenly, there are many spots around the globe where local lodges or chapters are part of a distant Grand Lodge or Chapter. A careful reading of many of these documents will reveal the notation "Masonic jurisdiction thereunto belonging" which allowed Grand Lodges and Chapters to have constituent members in distant points. Printed on fine vellum in Edinburgh and written in English, Latin and French.
Size: 24" x 18"

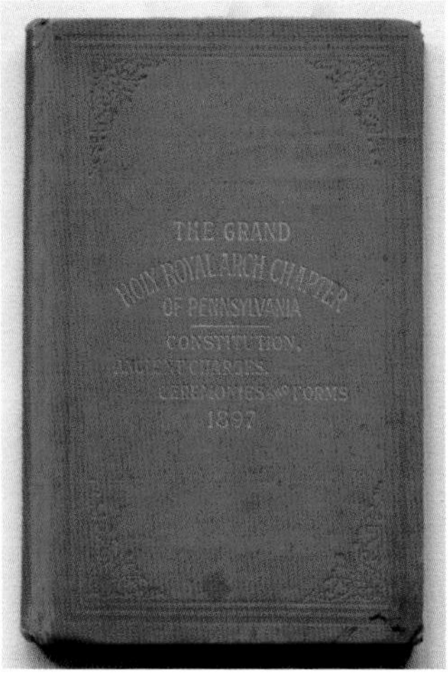

The General Grand Chapter for the United States, as well as many affiliated and unaffiliated State Grand Chapters, produced a regular digest of decisions and books of forms for local scribes/secretaries. This is an 1897 hardcover copy of the Pennsylvania Grand Chapter's book.

From the same book of constitutions, here is the officer's apron and crown and members' apron and crown worn during Royal Arch ceremonies.

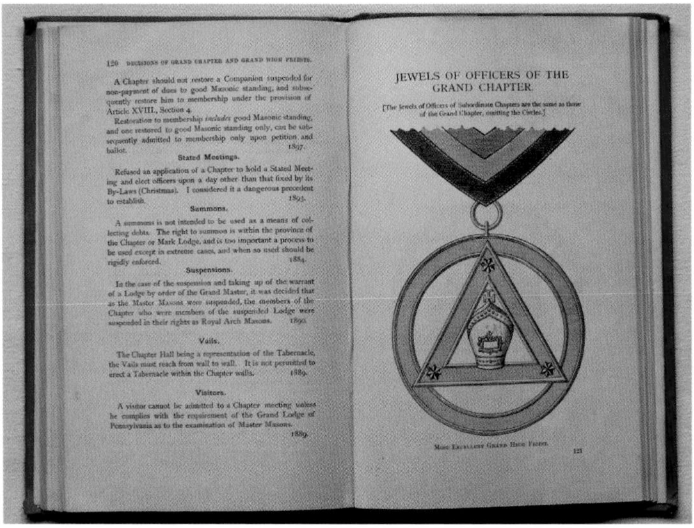

Shown here is the badge of the Grand High Priest under the Pennsylvania constitution.

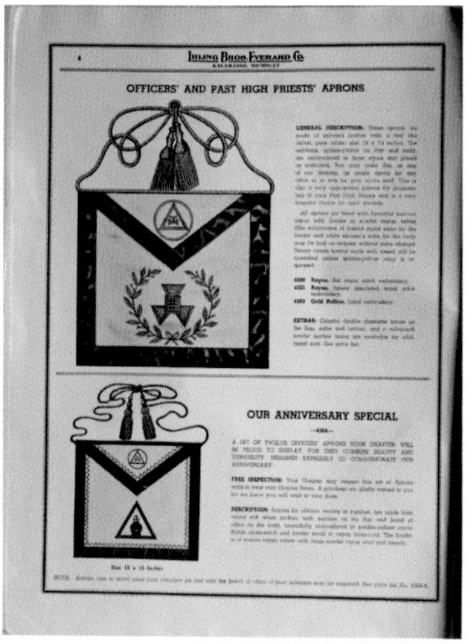

This image is taken from a 1960s trade catalog of Ihling Brothers Everard Company from Kalamazoo, Michigan. As one of the leading retailers of Royal Arch regalia in the country, their catalogs are an important resource in learning about the different styles of royal Arch regalia. Shown here are the medium-range-priced officers' aprons for Royal Arch Chapters. They are worked in rayon with gold embroidery.

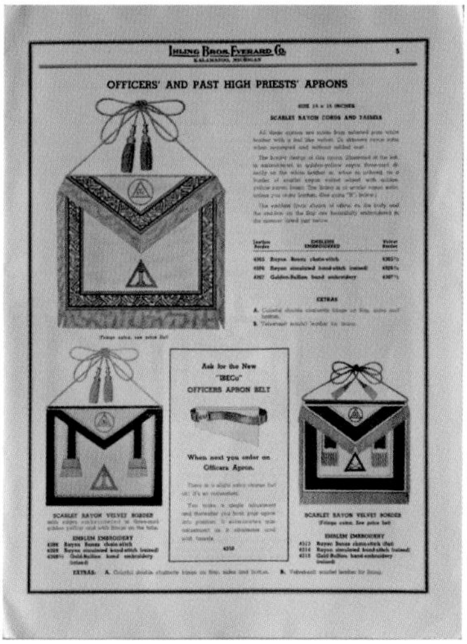

These aprons are more deluxe and include gold fringe taking the price up by several dollars.

piece. These tokens are among the mostly commonly found Masonic commemorative.

The regalia of the Royal Arch is somewhat complex to understand due in part to the complex governance structure. There is a General Grand Royal Arch Chapter for the United States although not all state Grand Chapters haven chosen to affiliate with this body. The consequences of these divisions are that there is a wide variety of Royal Arch jewels and aprons. Royal Arch regalia is red in color distinguishing it from the

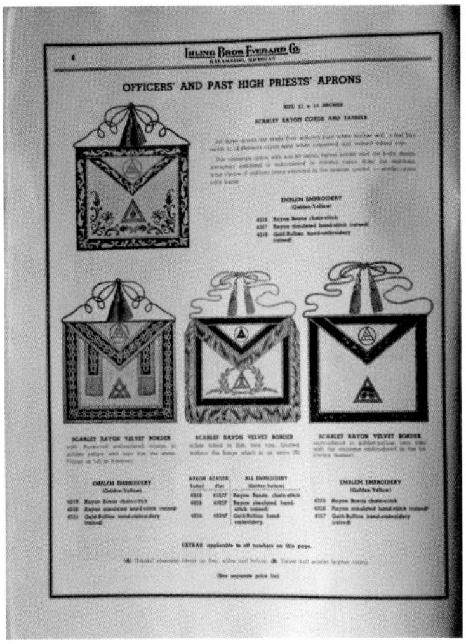

These aprons have embroidered borders which was permitted in some but not all jurisdictions.

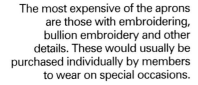

The most expensive of the aprons are those with embroidering, bullion embroidery and other details. These would usually be purchased individually by members to wear on special occasions.

blue of Lodges, the purple of the Royal and Select Masons or the black of the Knights Templar.

In the General Grand Chapter of the United States and its constituent members, Past High Priest (past presiding officer) jewels are usually small gold pins with enamel and jewel work. In unaffiliated states, such as Pennsylvania, the jewels are much simpler and more restrained.

In the United Kingdom, it is customary for Royal Arch Masons to wear a breast jewel—often in gold or gold-washed-sterling—to show their membership. These Royal Arch jewels are of a similar design and style albeit that they can be made of a wide range of material. Such jewels are occasionally worn in the United States but without much regularity.

This photograph shows an English Royal Arch Mason in formal attire wearing his sash, apron, and jewel. Marked "S. Buist/ Liverpool" Size: 5" x 7"

Upon receiving the Mark Master Mason degree, the Royal Arch chapter generally presents a small token to the new member. It is then up to that member to have it engraved with the "mark" or personal symbol that he has chosen. Most do so with their own tools, as in this example, from a Northumberland Pennsylvania chapter. Size: 1 ½"

IV

Royal and Select Masons and the Knights Templar

The Royal and Select Masons, sometimes referred to as Cryptic Masonry, is a series of three degrees conferred between the Royal Arch Chapter and the Knights Templar Commandery. It is the smallest of the three bodies comprising the York Rite since membership in a Royal and Select Masons Council is not a requirement for advancement to the degree of Knights Templar. The color of the degree is a rich royal purple and all aprons and jewels are in that color.

Among the most colorful of all the fraternal groups are the Masonic Knights Templar whose elaborate regalia and ceremonies rank perhaps second only to the Shriners in terms of public knowledge of fraternal groups. Established in England in the 18th century, the Masonic Templars claim descent from the Medieval Poor Soldiers in Christ who were disbanded in 1314 by Pope Clement V and King Philip the Fair of France. The purported line of descent from the dissolution of the order in the 14th century progresses to Scotland where many Templars were thought to have escaped. The

Perhaps the most distinctive piece of Knights Templar regalia is the sword that all members have an option of acquiring. Patterned loosely on 19th century militia swords, there is an infinite number of varieties and makers for these. Common features to all are the Medieval allegorical engravings and castings, the name of the owner and his local commandery, and the cross and crown. This example belonged to Harley L. Swift, Pittsburgh Commander Number 11 and dates from the early 1920s. It was made by M.C. Lilley and Company. Size: 36"

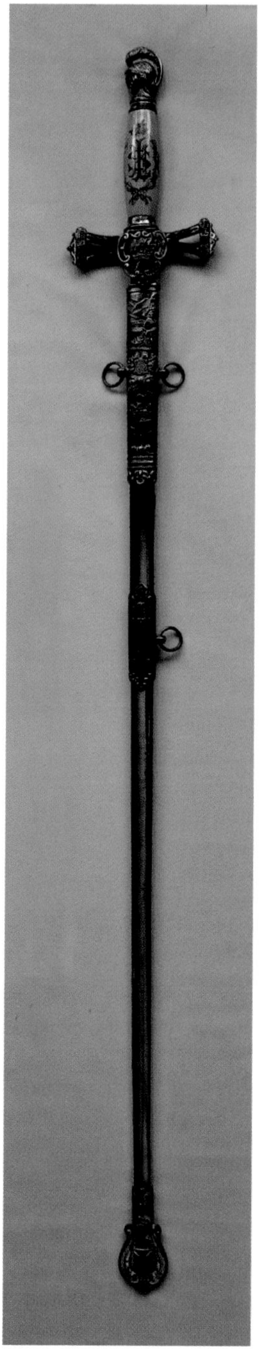

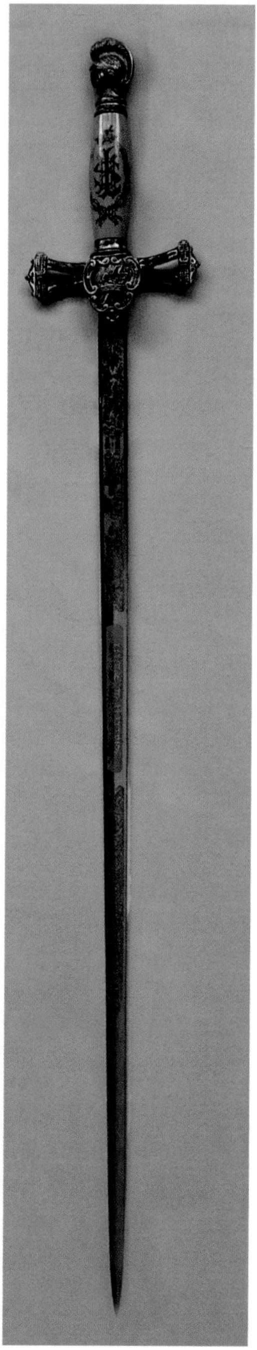

This young Knights Templar from Pittsburgh is wearing typical parade dress for the commandery. On his head is the chapeau with white plume. He wears the sash, sword belt, and sword that was regulation of the time. The leather gauntlets are no longer worn but were common in the late 19th century. They feature an applied red cross. The medal on his chest is probably one issued for attending a state or grand commandery session. Photographed by S.M. Robinson of Pittsburgh, circa 1890-91. Size: 4" x 7"

Order then descended in secret until joining with the stonemasons and freemasons to create the Masonic Knights Templars.

In the 19th century, the Masonic Knights Templars adopted a strong military flavor complete with drill teams and marching units. They are organized into local Commanderies, state Commanderies, and up

The Knights Templar of the 20th century wear a uniform that is loosely patterned on American military and firemen's coats of the turn of the century. Part of the regalia are the bullion shoulder straps with radiant crosses worn by all members. More elaborate examples are awarded to local, state and national officers.
Size: 4 ½"

to the Grand Commandery for the United States. Joining a Commandery usually leads the Mason into purchasing the elaborate uniform of the order. Today that consists of a black sports coat to which various insignia are attached. In the past, however, it was much more complex.

There were vast differences and changes in uniforms among the various Commanderies of the Knights Templar resulting in an almost infinite variety of regalia. Among the most elaborate were those worn in New England where frock coats, aprons with coin silver skulls and crossbones attached, leather

Wearing the undress uniform of the Knights Templar, this Knight has the baseball or forage-style cap that was popular in the late 19th century in many jurisdictions. His uniform has the shoulder straps with his commandery number embroidered on them. He wears a jewel on his chest, possibly that of a Past Commander. He carries his sword and is not wearing a belt or sash. This was staged deliberately for the photographer. Circa 1890.
Size: 4" x 6"

This image dates from the 1920s and shows a Grand Encampment of Pennsylvania event probably held in Carlisle, Pennsylvania. The two Templars on the right side of the photograph are dressed in the long frock coat that was regulation for the Knights Templars. The man on the far right wears the Knights of Malta cross on his chest as well as Past Commander's jewel and shoulder boards. The man on the left, probably the marshal for the event, wears only the Knights of Malta badge. Size: 8" x 10"

gauntlets and cuffs, and chests full of medals were the norm. In the early years, the skull and crossbones remained a popular motif appearing on much Templar regalia. However, by the end of the century, the cross and crown, was popular among many groups and had replaced the skull and crossbones. In order to distinguish the Masonic Knights Templars from other organizations who used the cross and crown, they added the Latin phrase *In Hoc Signo Vinces* ("In this Sign Conquer"). This is based upon the story of the Roman Emperor Constantine's conversion to Christianity.

All initiates into a Commandery of Knights Templars are also created Knights of Malta. Although historically these two crusading orders did not get along particularly well, in Masonic tradition their memberships are blended. During the ceremony, when creating a Knight of Malta, all candidates are given one of these highly stylized badges. Better quality examples with a vaulted cross and a suspension bar with the name of the state the member is a member in are available for a higher fee. Size: 4"

This is another variant member's medal jewel for the Knights of Malta. It features a stylized Maltese Cross with suspension bars engraved "Santa Monica Bay/No. 61/F.D. Battistini." Size: 5"

The degree of Knights Templar also carries with it a cross, although it is not common to see this in the United States. This example came from the Pacific Northwest and may be Canadian or American. It features the red cross of the Templars suspended from a red and white ribbon. Size: 5"

This New England Templar wears the full regalia of the order including sash, belt, gauntlets, sword, jewel, chapeau and apron. The Templar apron (triangular in form with applied skull and crossbones) appears to have been worn mostly in New England rather than further south. This photograph, dating from the 1880s illustrates the height of Templar regalia. The subject is identified as "Ira E. Woodward" of Lancaster, New Hampshire.
Size: 4" x 8"

This poignant photograph of two young boys dressed as Masonic Knights Templars appears to have a story connected to it. The reverse of the card notes that these are the two sons of the late Emminent Commander DeLester Sackett who died March 27, 1910, in Elgin, Illinois. Since the boys (identified as DeLester and DeForest) were too young to have been Masonic Templars, this regalia must have been custom ordered and made for them to wear in honor of their father. The older boy appears to be wearing his father's Past Commander's jewel although it is difficult to be certain.
Size: 5" x 8"

This is a typical Past Thrice Illustrious Master's jewel for a Council of Royal and Select Masons. The form is similar to that of a Royal Arch Past High Priest's jewel except that the central emblem is of a trowel, square, and depiction of the 47th Problem of Euclid. The latter is common to the Past Master of a Blue Lodge jewel. The ribbon is purple and the suspension bar has the name of the recipient engraved on it. The reverse is engraved "Presented to Ill. Companion Thurman F. Sallade, PTIM/by Creigh Council No. 16/R&SM Reading PA/ December 17, 1977." Size: 5"

The Masonic Knights Templar confers three degrees: Order of the Red Cross, Knights Templar, and Knight of Malta. After receiving all three degrees, one is then a full member of the Commandery and entitled to purchase and wear the regalia of membership. This includes the white enamel Maltese cross on black ribbon of the Knights of Malta. These crosses are extremely common and are often mistaken for military awards. A second cross, usually found in Canada and the UK but not the United States, is the red and white Knights Templar Cross. Finally, third is the distinctive badge for an individual local Commandery. These vary in quality and style from base metal examples to those with elaborate enamel and gold work.

A particularly complex and interesting subset of Commandery Regalia is the badges, plates, mugs, etc., produced for attending annual convocations of state or national encampments. These ran the gamut

This Nebraska Templar is wearing the sash, sword, belt, and chapeau of the Order along with gauntlets suggesting the image from the 1890s. The black handled sword is typical of the late 19th century. Beginning however around 1910, white handled swords came to replace the older style. Marked Bishoff/Wymote Nebraska.
Size: 5" x 7"

There are an almost infinite variety of Past Commander jewels for the Knights Templar. Some are made of gold, silver, and inset with rare gems. In the late 20th century, when such materials became prohibitively expensive, plating and other more cost-effective pieces were made. This is a Past Commander's cross from DeMolay Commandery, No. 9. The reverse is engraved "Presented to Sir Knight Richard E. Kaudenslager/ Commander/1979-80." Size: 4 ½"

from well-made and beautiful to tinny and cheap. Photographs of Commandery members frequently show them decked out like Christmas trees as they wear the various commemorative badges produced for annual state and national encampments.

A final and important area of Templar regalia is the sword. A cursory look at eBay will show a staggering number of Templar swords—new and old—being offered for sale. These swords were, and still are, being produced in wide ranges of quality for sale to members. The form is uniformly consistent and derived from 19th century bandsmen and militia swords. The owner then could embellish them with chain guards, blade engraving, and elaborate pommels. Rank and file members wear silver swords while past Commanders are entitled to gold-washed swords.

This sharp image of a Templar in the 1890s shows us a clear detail of how the sword was attached to the sword belt. One hanger is shown close to the buckle while the second appears to be attached behind the sash or baldric. Some Templar sword belts also had a hook for the sword to fit into the bottom of sash or baldric thereby allowing it to ride higher and more safely. Marked "Bairstow/Warren Pa." and dating circa 1890.
Size: 4" x 7"

This stately gentleman wears the full regalia of the Knights Templar including frock coat, sash, chapeau, sword and belt. He wears the Knights of Malta Cross, his Commandery membership medal, and a badge for attending the Grand Commandery sessions in Saratoga Springs, New York. The photo dates from the first decades of the 20th century. On is chest is Knights of Malta cross, a Commandery jewel, and the badge for attending Grand Commandery sessions in Saratoga Springs New York.
Size: 5" x 8"

V

The Scottish Rite

The Ancient and Accepted Scottish Rite is among the best known and most misunderstood of the Masonic rites or series of degrees. Founded in the late 18th or early 19th centuries, the AASR brings together a series of 33 degrees that it confers sequentially by several closely joined bodies. Membership is open to all members of Blue Lodges who are willing to pay the initiation fee, be balloted upon, and sit through a weekend of select presentations of various degrees. At the conclusion of the weekend, one is then invested as Sovereign Prince of the Royal Secret, which is the 32nd degree. Membership conveys neither rank nor prestige in a Blue Lodge and is simply another series of degrees and related rituals that a Master Mason can opt to join.

The 33rd degree, oft touted in literature, is reserved for a limited number of men. The active members of this degree are those men who govern the Scottish Rite. Those who are elected as leadership of the Scottish Rite at the state or national level are named as Active Members of the 33rd Degree. A much larger body are those men who are given the Honorary 33rd

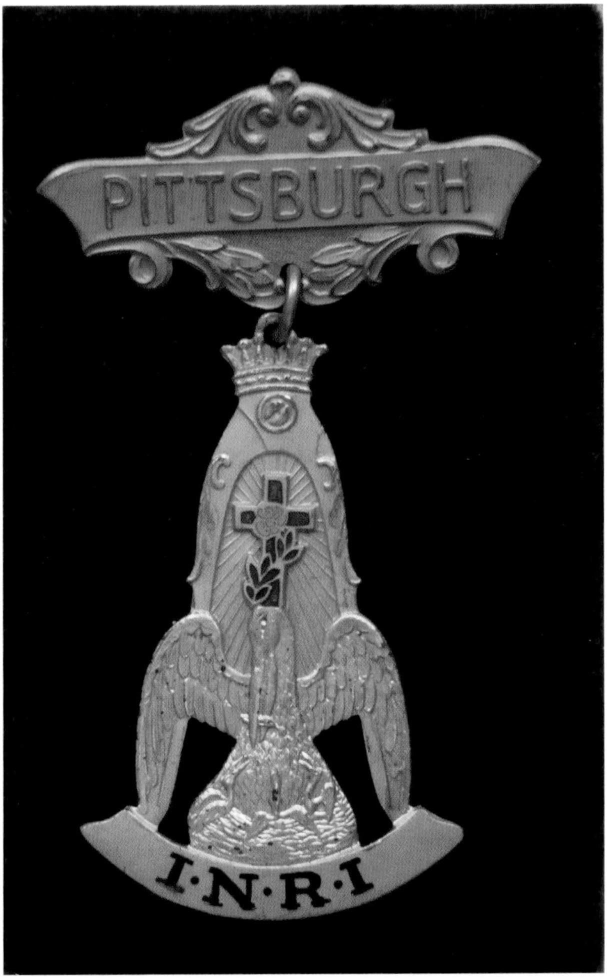

When joining the Scottish Rite (usually over the course of a long weekend), members witness a selection of certain degrees while others are conferred in name only. One degree, the eighteenth degree or Prince of the Rose Croix, is always conferred. Interestingly, in that while the Scottish Rite is open to men of all religious faiths, this particular degree does have overt Christian symbolism. Upon receiving that degree, in some jurisdictions, the new member is given a small breast jewel of this degree. The jewel depicts the mother pelican tearing open her own breast to feed her hungry children. This is symbolic of the idea of total sacrifice and is a common Christian religious belief. Given to Harley L. Swift upon joining the Scottish Rite in the Valley of Pittsburgh, 1921.
Size: 4"

This is a Scottish Rite member's medal from the Albany Consistory. It features the red cross and double-headed eagle badge of the Scottish Rite. It is pinned to a leatherette pocket protector so that it could be easily worn without damaging the wearer's suit coat. Size: 3"

Degree in recognition of their service to Freemasonry and humanity. This is given for outstanding Masonic and civic contributions.

In the United States, the Scottish Rite is divided into two separate and independent jurisdictions. The larger of the two, the AASR Southern Jurisdiction, has control of the Scottish Rite degrees in the South, Midwest, and Western United States. The AASR Northern Jurisdiction has control of the Scottish Rite degrees in New England and parts of the Mid-Atlantic and Midwest. Both have the same basic sequencing of degrees but there are ritualistic and administrative variations within. The AASR Northern Jurisdiction is the smaller and more reserved of the two bodies.

In other Scottish Rite jurisdictions, it is common to award a medal at the time of initiation to the 32nd degree. This small cross with the double-headed eagle and the number 32 in the middle was awarded circa 1930 to an unknown Mason whose initials BRH are engraved on the reverse.
Size: 4"

Scottish Rite regalia is not commonly seen and the officers rarely participate in public ceremonies so there are relatively few chances to view their regalia. Members' regalia are generally broken out into two categories. First are the medals given at the time of initiation in the Rite. These are usually either for the 18th (Knight of the Rose Croix) or 32nd (Sovereign Prince of the Royal Secret) degrees. They are not often worn after the initiation. The second form of regalia is the rings and lapel pins with the double-headed eagle of the Rite centered in the middle. These are very popular and commonly seen.

VI

Shrine, Red Cross of Constantine and Others

Little boys play cowboys and Indians and grown men play Saracen and Infidel. So began a popular and cynical description of the Ancient Arabic Nobles of the Mystic Shrine. Membership in either the York or Scottish rites along with Blue Lodge membership is the prerequisite qualification to becoming a Shriner. Founded in the late 19th century, the Shrine is one of several fun and philanthropic Masonic organizations founded to provide more socializing and less ritual for Freemasons.

The most distinctive piece of Shrine regalia is the fez that all members purchase and wear to various occasions. These are usually bejeweled with the name of the Temple that the Shriner belongs to as well as whatever internal "units" that he may be involved with including clowns, car club, etc. In addition, service as a present officer in the "Imperial Divan" is noted on the front of the fez. Finally, the presiding officer of a Shrine is known as the Imperial Potentate. Past and present Potentates have their title permanently bejeweled on their fezzes.

If a Mason has served as the presiding officer of all four York Rite bodies—a Blue Lodge, Royal Arch Chapter, a Council of Royal and Select Masons, and a Knights Templar Commandery—then he can be elected as a Knight of the York Rite Cross of Honor. The badge for this group consists of a braided neck cordon (being braided of the colors of all four bodies) from which hangs a crown pendant inset with miniatures of the past officer jewels for all four bodies. For Masons who are elected to Grand office in the York Rite and who also have been elected as Cross of Honor recipients, there is a next-level designation known as the Knight Grand Cross of the York Rite. If one serves as head of one grand body, then the distinction is known as first quadrant. Service as head of two grand bodies would be two quadrants and so forth.
Size: 1 ½"

The Tall Cedars of Lebanon is one of the most widespread of the various fun Masonic organizations. Founded for Master Masons, it is noted for its distinctive pyramidal headgear thought to be reminiscent of the cedar trees in Lebanon. This image shows the Quitapahilla Cedars from Lebanon County, Pennsylvania, marching in a parade in Atlantic City, New Jersey in 1928. The hand-colored image was probably produced to sell back to the subjects as a souvenir.
Size: 8" x 13"

Freemasonry has sprouted numerous side orders and bodies based upon a wide range of Biblical and romantic tales. Most date from the 19th century and are by invitation only. Some, such as the Red Cross of Constantine, are open solely to members based upon achievement within Freemasonry. Membership is by invitation only. Others like the Mystic Order of the Veiled Prophets and the Tall Cedars were founded strictly in the 20th century solely as fun and philanthropic organizations. Membership in these groups is open to all applying Master Masons.

This striking cabinet card was taken by the Schwentner firm of New York City and shows Noble John L. Wiegand, a member of Mecca Shrine, Ancient Arabic Order of the Nobles of the Mystic Shrine. Undated, but probably from the late 1880s, it is one of the earliest images of a Shriner wearing his fez. The fez is still worn to the present although modern examples are more elaborate in their decoration. Size: 5" x 7"

One of the many invitational bodies open to Master Masons is the Knights of the Red Cross of Constantine. The body derives its name from the story of the Roman Emperor Constantine who converted to Christianity and received a sign from God to engrave the cross on the shields of his men. By thus doing so, his men were assured of victory in combat. The Order has a following in the United States and awards a jewel to past "Sovereigns" or presiding officers. This example is engraved on the reverse "Sov. Edward H. Walker/St. James Conclave/1984-84."
Size: 1 ½"

Each year the Shriners hold an annual convention somewhere in the United States. For those attending, there are small medals produced for wear during the meeting. This example was produced for the 1950 Imperial Session held in California.
Size: 3"

With the Shrine, there is a small elective body that is dedicated to fun and humor. This is the Royal Order of Jesters. The badge is an enameled and colorful pendant with the initials ROJ and the number of the Court (local body). It is suspended from a purple satin ribbon.
Size: 1"

This striking plate was made to commemorate the building of the first Shrine temple in Harrisburg, Pennsylvania. The decorative border shows numerous serious and humorous shrine elements while the central image is that of the interior of the building. Interestingly, the credit for the interior is given to the architectural firm—W. F. Wise—that designed the space.
Size: 12"

VII

DeMolay

In terms of their regalia, probably the Order of DeMolay is among the most complex and fascinating. Founded as a training ground for future Freemasons, DeMolay has flourished where many other youth organizations (the Order of the Builders—also for Masonic youth or the Knights of Dunamis—for Boy Scouts) have disappeared. Frank Sherman Land and nine boys established the organization in Kansas City, Missouri, in 1919. The organization grew rapidly and has demonstrated remarkable survival skills where other groups have been unsuccessful. This is part and parcel due to the Order's ability to be nimble when it comes to embracing new technology and change. Early membership classes were broadcast on the radio while recently social networking has become the rage amongst its members.

The organization's regalia is easy to date insofar as the member pin has gone through three substantial changes. The earliest form dates from 1919 and was modified slightly in 1920. It lasted until 1932 when a second style was introduced. The third style pin came about in 1949 and remains in use today. Dating the emblem is even easier insofar that there were 10

This DeMolay Past Master Councilor's Jewel is particularly an interesting study. The pin hanging from the jewel is a first-style member's pin suggesting that the owner, "Jim Russell," was Master Councilor of Wm. F. Ewing Chapter (probably Texas). However, the ribbon is not the black and white bi-color stock ribbon that was regulation for the early jewels. A closer look shows that the top and middle bars appear to be more recent than the bottom. So, we are left with the mystery of whether this was an old jewel that was re-ribboned or possibly the entire piece is made up of parts from several jewels.
Size: 3" x 1 ¼"

Until the late 20th century, most members of the Order of DeMolay would purchase a member medal to wear to meetings and at public occasions. The earliest of these medals were numbered on the reverse as they were issued by the then Grand Council for the Order of DeMolay. This example is numbered "4314" on the reverse. What makes this example so interesting is the black and white grosgrain ribbon. This is not a regulation ribbon and appears to have been added later. Black and white ribbons were used for Past Master Councilor jewels so it is possible that the member re-ribboned his member's medal after he served as Master Councilor of his local chapter. Size; 4" x 1 ½"

All DeMolay members usually acquire a member pin to be worn on the shirt under the jacket or coat like a college fraternity pin. This example is a first-style member pin and is dated on the reverse 1921. It has a small chain and pin guard to prevent it from being lost. Surrounding the central shield are the ten pearls commemorating the founding nine members and Frank S. Land, the adult founder of the Order.
Size: ½"

pearls surrounding the central motif for each of the 9 original members and the tenth being for the founder. As each died, a pearl was replaced by a ruby (today there being ten rubies). However, there is a caveat to this in that old regalia stocks were frequently used up so that out of period items can often be found.

DeMolay has a complex system of awards and medals given to its members, both active and senior, as well as to outsiders. Active members can earn merit bars that hang from a suspension drop, bring in new members to win the Founder's Membership Award or Blue Honor Key, and work to become a Representative DeMolay. All of these have awards that have their own regalia and insignia that has changed and evolved over the years.

DeMolay also provides jewels for their past presiding officers, scribes (secretaries) and treasurers.

These two Past Master Councilor Meritorious Service Awards illustrate not only changes in time for DeMolay regalia, but also the personalizing efforts of many members. The MSA is still given to a Past Master Councilor who meets and exceeds a set list of criteria for their work. This pair of pins is from a single member, Stephen Meidy, who received the silver one in 1929 and the gold one in 1930. Today, the award is only given once and in gold whereas in the early years it could be given in two metals for the first and second awards. The medallion is the first style pin.
Size: 2" x 1"

The Past Master Councilor's jewel is one of two types. The older style, usually with a gold or gold wash to it, was the more expensive jewel and given by more affluent chapters. The second style is simpler and cost less and thus was given by less wealthy chapters. In addition, there is a unique merit system for outstanding service as a chapter's Master Council (presiding officer). The Past Master Councilor Meritorious Service Award is given for particularly exemplary service as a Master Councilor. In addition to these awards for local leadership, there are also jewels given for service as district, state, and International officers.

This Past Master Councilor's jewel was probably made in the last twenty years. Interestingly, DeMolay had an exclusive relationship with Balfour International to produce its regalia. However, issues regarding quality and availability of some items led a slew of other makers to attempt to produce regalia. This jewel is marked "Made in Taiwan" on the reverse and is slightly longer than the jewels produced by Balfour.
Size: 4 1/4" x 1 ½"

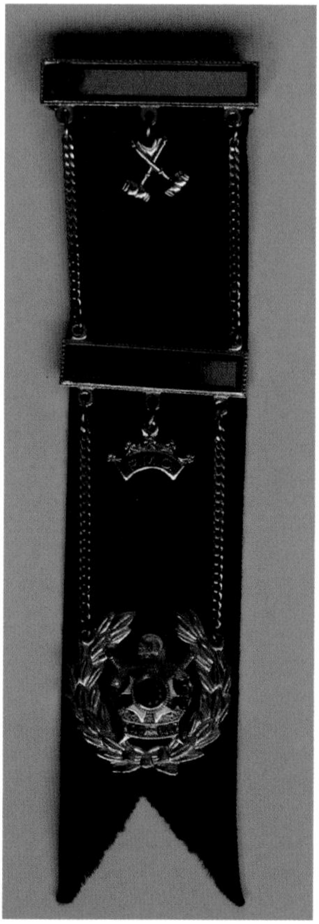

DeMolay merit bars were, and still are, issued to members by their local chapters based upon the fulfillment of certain tasks or duties. Much like the patches of the boy scouts, merit bars were given for excellence in school, attending meetings, civic service, etc. They could be given multiple times with the basic bar in white and continuing up to the gold bar for being awarded five times. The "Merit" merit bar is unusual in that there are not specific criteria for awarding this. In some chapters, it is given for the highest service to the local chapter and is often worn separately from other merit bars. This example is on a second-style member pin drop and dates from the 1930s.
Size: 4" x 1 ½"

DeMolay sports teams were, and still remain, an important part of the organization's mission. This team, probably from Chambersburg, Pennsylvania, is wearing the first-style member's insignia on their uniforms. The photograph is dated 1926.
Size: 8"x 10"

For active members, the highest honor is the Degree of Chevalier (French for the word Knight) that is rarely given and then only for the highest achievements in the Order and to the community. For a time, in the 1950s and 1960s, it was considered the hardest of all youth awards to obtain trumping even the Eagle Scout. The degree's regalia includes a neck medal (originally hung from a wide collar and now from yellow cordage) and a finger ring (silver or gold).

A second hierarchy exists for adult advisors and their honors that begins with the Cross of Honor given for service after three years as an advisor, followed

The Cross of Honor is an award given to advisors for superior service after three years. The Cross was originally awarded as a breast medal then it became a neck decoration and then back to being a chest decoration. Such changes in DeMolay regalia make it among the most interesting areas to collect. This is a neck cross probably from the 1950-60 period. The central pin has three red rubies and the rest are pearls, suggesting an early date although regalia stocks were often used long after changes were made. The red grosgrain ribbon has faded a bit, but it still retains its original sizing buckle. Originally, and today, this ribbon would have been two-tone.
Size: 1 ½"

This is a second-style Cross of Honor dating from the 1930s. It is mounted, as were all DeMolay adult awards in this period, as a breast medal rather than a neck pendant. The two tone ribbon was used on all advisor medals.
Size: 4" x 1 ½"

The active Legion of Honor is the highest adult award for service to humanity and the order. This is a post World War II-era piece. The active Legion has a red neck cordon and blue cross. The honorary Legion, given to adults who were not members of the order as young men, has a white cordon and cross. The original Legion of Honor was worn as a breast medal but then, in the post-war period, it shifted over to a neck cordon. This example is somewhat heavier than most and suggests an early manufacture. Size: 4" x 2"

by the Legion of Honor (paralleling the degree of Chevalier but for adults only), the rarely given Guild of the Leather Apron (Advisor of the Year), and lastly (paralleling the Scottish Rite) election as Active/ Honorary Member of the International Supreme Council. Like the youth awards, the regalia has gone through numerous changes over the years.

The degree of Chevalier (French for Knight) is the highest honor given to an active member of the Order of DeMolay. The medal is a simple bronzed pendant of Jacques DeMolay, namesake of the Order, in a red enamel wreath. The original medal was awarded on a wide collar with a patch of the member's insignia at the point just above the hanging pendant. Today, the medal hangs from yellow cords. In addition to the collar and pendant, there is also a matching ring in either silver or gold worn on the ring finger of the left hand.
Size: 3" x 2"

DeMolay has also sprouted several side degrees or groups as the order attempted to copy the more complex rites of adult Masonic bodies. The Chivalric Knights of the Holy Order of the Fellow Soldiers of Jacques DeMolay (shortened to "Priory") is one such body that is now almost extinct. It has a quasi Knights Templar flavor to it. In addition, local chapters also often created special bodies, groups and rituals unique to them.

VIII

Women's Masonic Groups

While women have been, and continue to be, strictly prohibited from becoming Freemasons, there has arisen a parallel track of organizations that are quasi-Masonic and open to the wives, daughters, sisters, and friends of members. For adult women, there is the Order of the Eastern Star, which is probably the largest of the female bodies. Membership in this group thereby opens the door to join the Order of the Amaranth that has a quasi Knights Templar feel and the White Shrine of

The Cross of Color is the highest honor that an active Rainbow or adult advisor can receive. It is a small base metal pendant suspended from a purple neck ribbon. They are not often engraved and the styling has changed very little, so dating examples in nearly impossible.
Size: 2"

ABOVE AND THE FOLLOWING PAGE:
These are all individual jewels from a large and complete set of Eastern Star officer jewels. In OES, there are three types of officer jewels. The colored triangles are for the five star points of the "Eastern Star." The starred jewels with enamel are for the elected Worthy Patron, Matron, Assistant Patron and Assistant Matron. The jewels were originally hung from silk ribbons but at some point they were replaced with identical long gold chains.
Size: 2"

Jerusalem, which parallels the Ancient Arabic Nobles of the Mystic Shrine.

The Eastern Star is open to men and women although each state has its own rules about membership. Presiding over an Eastern Star Chapter are the Worthy Patron and Worthy Matron. There are small gold and diamond pins that were produced for both the Past Worthy Matron and the Past Worthy Patron of a local Eastern Star Chapter. Interestingly, unlike their male counterparts, the formal regalia of these women's groups is limited with even the past presiding officer pins being somewhat small (although often set with diamonds to add some glitter).

There are two unrelated organizations for young girls that connect them to the Masonic fraternity in general and the Order of the Eastern Star in particular. Smaller of the two are the Job's Daughters. Founded in 1920, it is restricted to girls who have a Masonic family member. Locally, it is presided over by the Honored Queen. It does not have an extensive honors system and appears to grant only one honor degree—that of the Degree of Royal Purple.

The Order of the Rainbow for Girls has an award system loosely patterned on DeMolay and scouting. The illustrated pin (missing its wreath around the pot of gold at the bottom) is worn on a small strip of cloth pinned to a Rainbow Girls dress. Known as a brag rag, it is where Rainbow Girls display their various service pins. The bars were awarded for civic and Masonic service and girls earned them in various progressions. Size: 5"

The larger of the two groups is the International Order of the Rainbow for Girls founded in 1922. Unlike the Job's Daughters, Rainbow Girl membership is open to all girls between 11 and 20. Locally, it is presided over by the Worthy Advisor. It has a more complex system of awards, etc., than the Job's Daughters. This includes service pins worn on a small strip of cloth pinned to the white dress that all officers are required to wear. Known as the brag rag, it also is where a Past Worthy Advisor would also wear her pin.

The Order has one honor that is given to members and advisors—the Grand Cross of Color. The form of the cross has not substantially changed over the years and thus it is nearly impossible to determine ages of regalia.

The Order of Job's Daughters has perhaps the least amount of regalia of all the organizations with Masonic ties. Illustrated here is the pin which is worn by all members of the Order. It is a simple triangle with the emblem of the Order in the center. A chain guard and second pin keep it from being lost if the first catch comes un-done.
Size: ¾"

IX

Prince Hall Masonry

The history of Prince Hall or African-American Freemasonry is a fascinating story within the larger scope of fraternal organizations. English Masonry, while predominantly for whites, did not directly prohibit others from joining. In India, for example, it is said that Brother Rudyard Kipling was initiated by a Muslin, Hindu, and Christian respectively. However, in the United States, the color line appears to have been established early and remains to the present.

Prince Hall, a former slave, lived in Massachusetts and was initiated as a Freemason by a British lodge

This is an officer's cap of the Prince Hall affiliation of the Scottish Rite. The dove is usually the badge of the messenger or deacon. This pillbox cap is made of this satin, gold bullion wire and embroidery. Circa 1950s.
Size: 14"

This photograph shows the members of DeMolay Consistory (Prince Hall Affiliation) of the Scottish Rite in Philadelphia holding a banquet to honor several of their members. The individual members wear the black pillbox cap that is distinctive to the 32nd degree of the Scottish Rite. At the head table, the officers wear more elaborate examples of this same cap in yellow as well as black. The image is dated 1965. Size: 24"

prior to the American Revolution. Hall brought together a number of his friends and established the first "African" lodge in America. From this came the present system of lodges collectively known as Prince Hall Masonry. Sadly, the existing white lodges declined to acknowledge the existence of the black lodges in their respective states on the grounds that only one lodge could occupy a given state or colony at a period. While this was not true in Europe, American lodges enforced this rule, and as a result, the Prince Hall system evolved completely independently.

The Prince Hall lodges are identical to the degree structures of the white lodges including the Scottish Rite, York Rite, Shrine, and other bodies. A youth organization called the Knights of Pythagoras was similar in its appeal to the Order of DeMolay. Today there are Grand Lodges of Prince Hall masons throughout the United States. The regalia of the Prince Hall lodges is very similar and can

Shown here are the officers of Hiram Lodge in Detroit, Michigan, in the 1960s. The officers wear typical Prince Hall officer collars consisting of links with various Masonic emblems from which hangs the pendant of their office. The aprons are fringed and painted with the badge of their respective office.
Size: 8" x 10"

be distinguished by the inclusion of the phrase "Prince Hall" somewhere on the badge. Also, Prince Hall Grand Lodges frequently utilize metal chains stitched to cloth collars as badges of both current and past rank.

The exciting news is that within the last several years, fraternal recognition—long denied by the white lodges to the Prince Hall lodges—has now been extended. As a result, there are close-working ties between the various bodies and even shared meeting spaces in some jurisdictions.

X

Odd Fellows

Next to Freemasonry, the largest of the historic fraternal groups in America was the Odd Fellows. The roots of Odd Fellowship can be traced back to England where it was established during the 18th century. Its colorful name has been interpreted any number of ways. One suggestion

The Odd Fellows have several auxiliary bodies. This small jewel is for a Past Loyal Patron of the Ladies Auxiliary of the Patriarchs Militant. The Patriarchs Militant is an additional degree of the Odd Fellows. Like the Knights Templar, it has a strong military flavor and membership in an Odd Fellows lodge is required in order to belong to a local "Canton." This pin is for the Idaho Auxiliary to Canton No. 25.
Size: 2 1/2"

Shown here is a Past Noble Grand of the Odd Fellows. He is wearing a finely embroidered collar which has a closer consisting of the three rings of odd fellowship and the hand within the star badge of his past rank. The image was taken by H.D. Garnes of Philadelphia and dates from 1879-1890.
Size: 5" x 7"

This carte de visite shows an unknown man wearing the collar and badge of a State Grand Master (probably Pennsylvania). The beautifully embroidered and fringed collar is closed by three rings and the star with hand in the center pendant which denotes the Past Grand rank. Taken by Stockton Stokes working at 43 North Eighth Street in Philadelphia between 1877 and 1882.
Size: 3" x 2"

The small cake on the pedestal in the foreground suggests that these rather serious-looking men are gathered to celebrate the anniversary of their Odd Fellow's lodge. Note the wide range of collars and sashes being worn by the members. The more elaborate examples in the foreground are past Noble Grands of their lodge. Circa 1950. Size: 8" x 10"

is that Odd Fellowship appealed to workingmen as opposed to the white-collar workers who joined the Freemasons. Thus, they came to think of themselves as being the odd fellows.

A second story told is that an English journalist observed that he found it odd to see fellows rather then the rich helping widows and orphans. The benevolence of the Odd Fellows remains to the present and support this story.

In England, during the 18th and 19th centuries, there were several different competing Grand Lodges of Odd Fellowship. Like the Masonic fraternity, these different Grand Lodges began chartering subordinate

lodges overseas. In the United States, the first Odd Fellows lodge was established in Baltimore under the affiliation of the English Manchester Unity of Odd Fellows. In 1842, the Baltimore lodges separated from the English grand lodge and became a separate sovereign body. Concurrent with this action was the chartering in New York by the Manchester Unity of Odd Fellows of a second lodge reserved for blacks. That lodge, still under the authority of the Manchester Unity of Odd Fellows, was the founding of the present day Grand United Order of Odd Fellows (GUOFF).

The Independent Order of Odd Fellows established, in 1851, a women's organization known as the Daughters of Rebekah that was open to both sexes. The Daughters wear a distinctive pink and green collar.

The men shown here are all Odd Fellow officers. The triangular pendants are the badges of rank for a local lodge, while the more elaborate collar is that worn by a District Deputy whose job is to oversee a region. Circa 1920.
Size: 8" x 10"

A third body, the Patriarchs Militant, was founded along the lines of the Masonic Knights Templar.

The Odd Fellows symbols include the three co-joined rings with the initials FLT for Fraternity, Love, and Truth. The rings are often colored red, white, and blue. The Patriarchs Militant utilized a stylized tent as their badge and the Rebekahs have their distinctive pink and green color scheme.

Within their lodge meetings, and occasionally for ceremonial public occasions, Odd Fellows members and officers wear elaborate distinctive collars. Much like the Masonic aprons, these cloth collars have become the hallmarks of Odd Fellowship and were usually depicted on early photographs of members. The colors and amount of embroidery usually distinguish the rank of the member.

Most fraternal organizations have a local, district, state, and national hierarchy of officers. This small pin made of bright cut metal is for a Past District Deputy Grand Master of the Odd Fellows. The symbolism includes the all-seeing eye of God on top and the scales of justice in the middle of the pendant. Size: 3"

Past and present presiding officers at the district and grand lodge levels are identified by elaborate gold collars. This example was awarded to Alfred Bridges, Past District Deputy Grand Master of District No. 22. The links of the collar are made up of the various emblems of Odd Fellowship including the three linked rings. Awarded collars such as this are not common to find insofar as the owner's family was usually required to return them after the death of the recipient. Size: 24"

The three interlocking rings of Odd Fellowship is perhaps the most distinctive badge of the Order. It can be found in nearly every media from tombstone carvings to simple silk commemorative ribbons such as this. Size: 4 ½" x 3"

Above and on preceding page: This is a partial set of Encampment officer's jewels. All are suspended from an embroidered ribbon. The various items symbolize the role of the various offices including inner and outer guard, secretary, etc. Several marked on the reverse "Supreme Lodge" suggesting that there was a degree of regulation of the issuing of these sets.
Size: 3" (average)

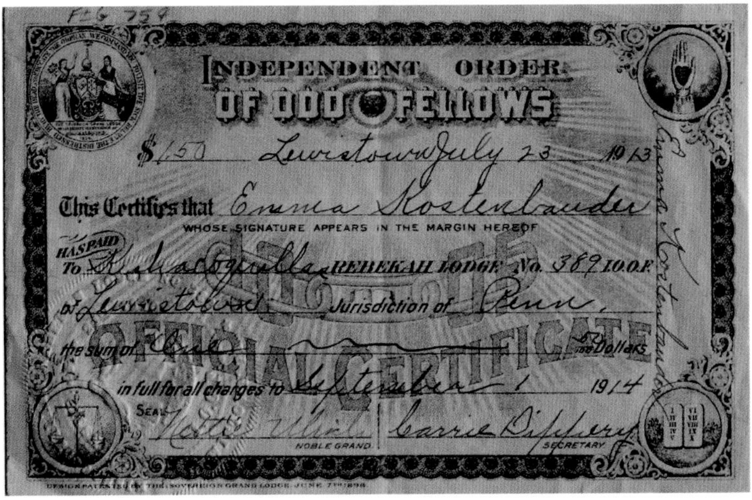

This is a simple membership certificate in the Odd Fellows. Produced on a small scale like this, they were intended to be carried in the wallet so that when traveling one could produce it to gain admission as a visitor.
Size: 5" x 4"

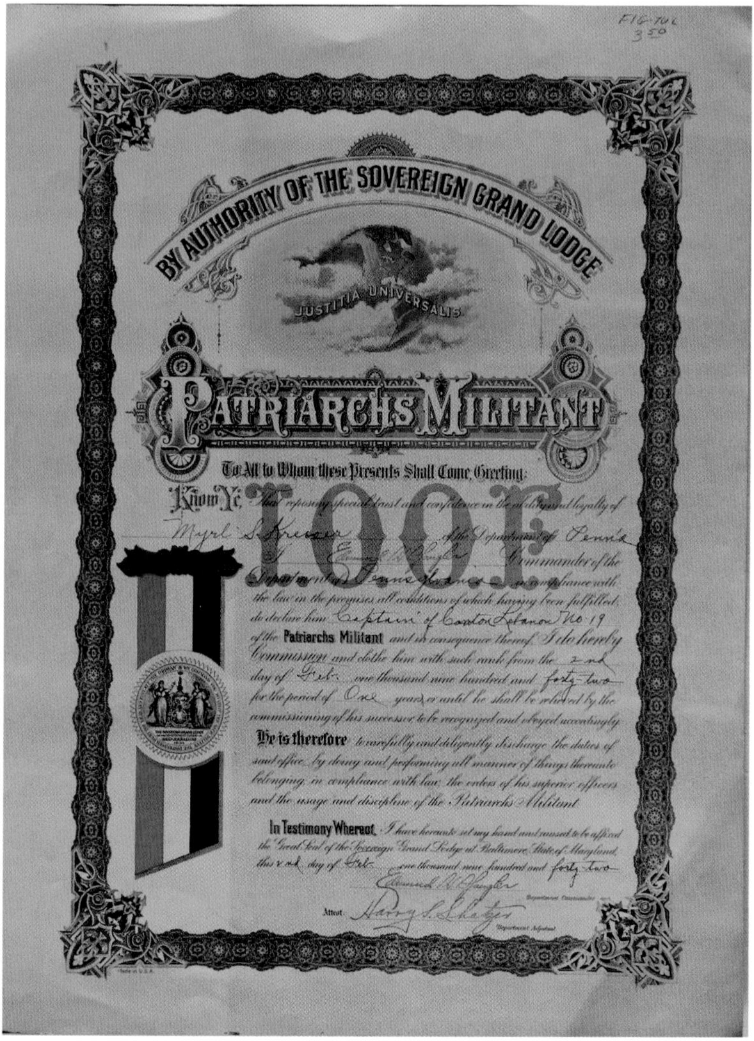

The Patriarchs Militant is an additional degree in the hierarchy of Odd Fellowship. This warrant (similar to a military commission) was signed by the department commander and was dated 1942. It appointed Myrl Kreiser as Captain of Canton Lebanon No. 19. Size: 20" x 24"

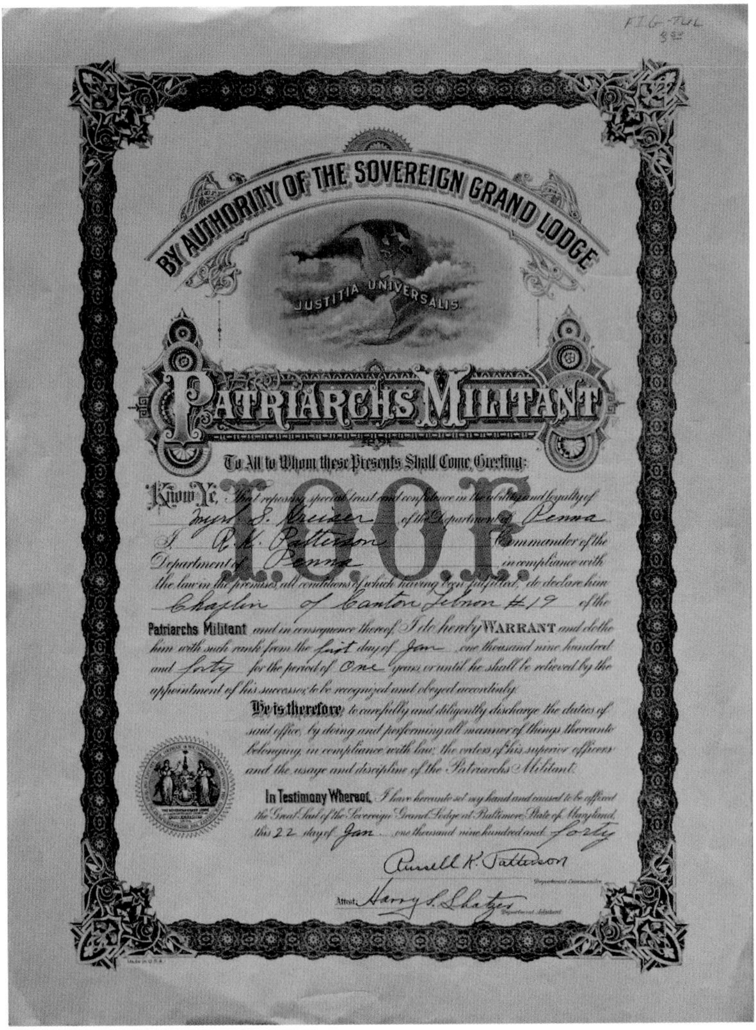

Less elaborate than the captain's warrant, this certificate appoints Myrl Kreiser as Chaplain of Canton Lebanon No. 19.
Size: 20" x 24"

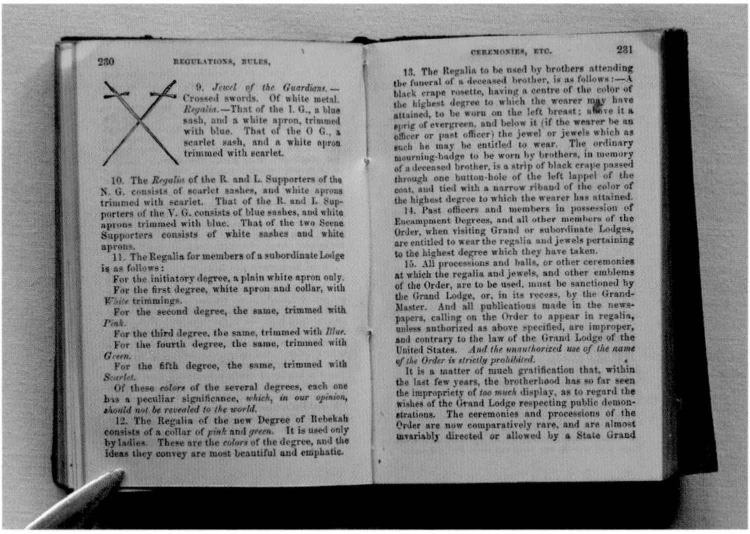

230 REGULATIONS, RULES,

9. *Jewel of the Guardians.*—Crossed swords. Of white metal. *Regalia.*—That of the I. G., a blue sash, and a white apron, trimmed with blue. That of the O G., a scarlet sash, and a white apron trimmed with scarlet.

10. The *Regalia* of the R. and L. Supporters of the N. G. consists of scarlet sashes, and white aprons trimmed with scarlet. That of the R. and L. Supporters of the V. G. consists of blue sashes, and white aprons trimmed with blue. That of the two Scene Supporters consists of white sashes and white aprons.

11. The Regalia for members of a subordinate Lodge is as follows:

For the initiatory degree, a plain white apron only.

For the first degree, white apron and collar, with *White* trimmings.

For the second degree, the same, trimmed with *Pink*.

For the third degree, the same, trimmed with *Blue*.

For the fourth degree, the same, trimmed with *Green*.

For the fifth degree, the same, trimmed with *Scarlet*.

Of these *colors* of the several degrees, each one has a peculiar significance, *which, in our opinion, should not be revealed to the world.*

12. The Regalia of the new Degree of Rebekah consists of a collar of *pink* and *green*. It is used only by ladies. These are the *colors* of the degree, and the ideas they convey are most beautiful and emphatic.

CEREMONIES, ETC. 231

13. The Regalia to be used by brothers attending the funeral of a deceased brother, is as follows:—A black crape rosette, having a centre of the color of the highest degree to which the wearer may have attained, to be worn on the left breast; above it a sprig of evergreen, and below it (if the wearer be an officer or past officer) the jewel or jewels which as such he may be entitled to wear. The ordinary mourning-badge to be worn by brothers, in memory of a deceased brother, is a strip of black crape passed through one button-hole of the left lappel of the coat, and tied with a narrow riband of the color of the highest degree to which the wearer has attained.

14. Past officers and members in possession of Encampment Degrees, and all other members of the Order, when visiting Grand or subordinate Lodges, are entitled to wear the regalia and jewels pertaining to the highest degree which they have taken.

15. All processions and balls, or other ceremonies at which the regalia and jewels, and other emblems of the Order, are to be used, must be sanctioned by the Grand Lodge, or, in its recess, by the Grand-Master. And all publications made in the newspapers, calling on the Order to appear in regalia, unless authorized as above specified, are improper, and contrary to the law of the Grand Lodge of the United States. *And the unauthorized use of the name of the Order is strictly prohibited.*

It is a matter of much gratification that, within the last few years, the brotherhood has so far seen the impropriety of *too much* display, as to regard the wishes of the Grand Lodge respecting public demonstrations. The ceremonies and processions of the Order are now comparatively rare, and are almost invariably directed or allowed by a State Grand

This page is from an Odd Fellow Companion dated 1867. Several items to note include the description of the sashes and aprons worn during the initiation as well as the regalia for the new Degree of Rebekah. The pink and green collar mentioned in the description of the degree is still worn today.

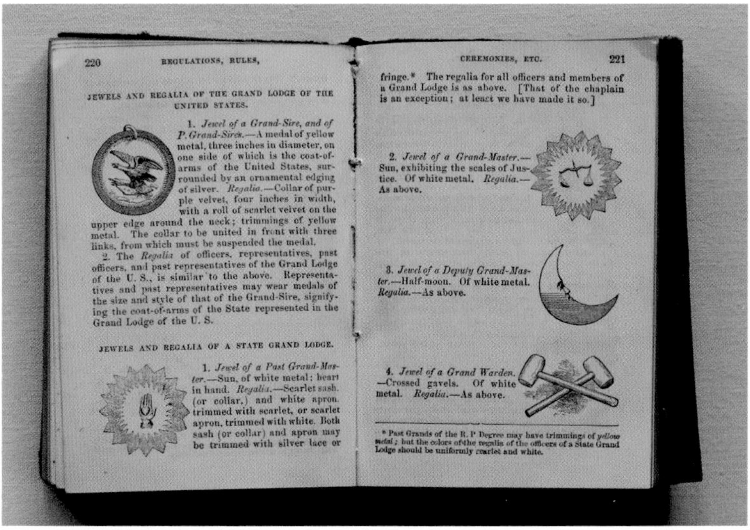

220 REGULATIONS, RULES,

JEWELS AND REGALIA OF THE GRAND LODGE OF THE UNITED STATES.

1. *Jewel of a Grand-Sire, and of P. Grand-Sires.*—A medal of yellow metal, three inches in diameter, on one side of which is the coat-of-arms of the United States, surrounded by an ornamental edging of silver. *Regalia.*—Collar of purple velvet, four inches in width, with a roll of scarlet velvet on the upper edge around the neck; trimmings of yellow metal. The collar to be united in front with three links, from which must be suspended the medal.

2. The *Regalia* of officers, representatives, past officers, and past representatives of the Grand Lodge of the U. S., is similar to the above. Representatives and past representatives may wear medals of the size and style of that of the Grand-Sire, signifying the coat-of-arms of the State represented in the Grand Lodge of the U. S.

JEWELS AND REGALIA OF A STATE GRAND LODGE.

1. *Jewel of a Past Grand-Master.*—Sun, of white metal; heart in hand. *Regalia.*—Scarlet sash, (or collar,) and white apron, trimmed with scarlet, or scarlet apron, trimmed with white. Both sash (or collar) and apron may be trimmed with silver lace or

CEREMONIES, ETC. 221

fringe.* The regalia for all officers and members of a Grand Lodge is as above. [That of the chaplain is an exception; at least we have made it so.]

2. *Jewel of a Grand-Master.*—Sun, exhibiting the scales of Justice. Of white metal. *Regalia.*—As above.

3. *Jewel of a Deputy Grand-Master.*—Half-moon. Of white metal. *Regalia.*—As above.

4. *Jewel of a Grand Warden.*—Crossed gavels. Of white metal. *Regalia.*—As above.

* Past Grands of the R. P. Degree may have trimmings of *yellow metal*; but the colors of the regalia of the officers of a State Grand Lodge should be uniformly scarlet and white.

Also from the Odd Fellow's Companion, this illustrates the badges of national and state officers. The heart and hand is an old emblem not necessarily unique to the Odd Fellows.

The Grand United Order of Odd Fellows was founded to serve the black community who were traditionally not admitted to membership by Odd Fellow lodges. This white cotton apron is transfer printed and incorporates the various emblems of Odd Fellowship including the all-seeing eye of God, scythe and sickle symbolizing time, and skull and crossbones for mortality and faith and justice. Probably late 19th century. Size: 14" x 12"

This pressed wood decorated box incorporates the emblem of the Encampment on the lid. Meeting in local Cantons, Encampment members follow a Masonic Knights Templar model. Their symbol is the tent with the all-seeing eye over the three links of odd fellowship. Size: 5" square

This is a graveyard flag produced nationally and distributed locally to be used on marking the graves of deceased Odd Fellows. It incorporates the three rings and all-seeing eye used on most Odd Fellow's regalia. Like veterans and other fraternal groups, the Odd Fellows regularly decorate the graves of their deceased members. Size: 12" x 8"

XI

Order of United American Mechanics

Founded in 1845 as the Union of Workers, the Order of United American Mechanics (OUAM) was perhaps the most widespread of nativist organizations in pre-Civil War America. Nativism is the political and social position of being anti-immigrant. In different eras, nativism focused its efforts upon various ethnic groups. In the founding years of OUAM, it was directed toward the Irish and Roman Catholics. By the end of the 19th century, it had shifted towards southern and east Europeans as well as anti-Semitism.

By1853, the order had grown so quickly that it established a second body known as the Junior Order of United American Mechanics or Jr. OUAM (JOUAM). Ironically, thanks to better membership and a focus upon insurance benefits, the Junior Order soon outpaced its parent to the extent that the OUAM disappeared completely by 1900.

The JOUAM soon evolved into an insurance and benefit society with a much less strongly nativist focus. Soon thereafter, women were admitted as members and many of the old OUAM membership

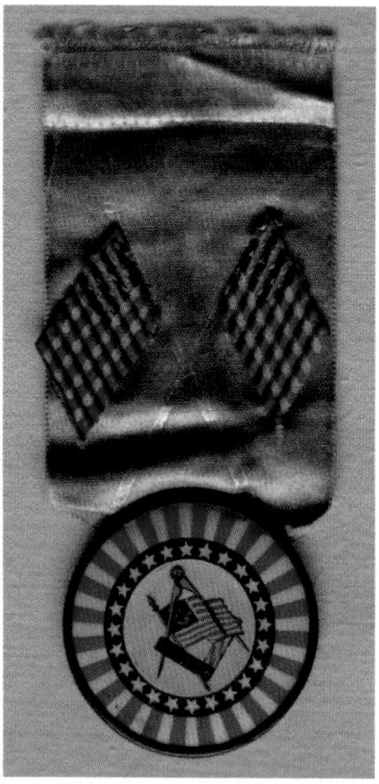

This celluloid badge and watered silk ribbon was probably part of a much larger piece worn by a member of the Junior Order of United American Mechanics. A quick look at this would lead most to assume that it was a Masonic badge insofar as the square and compass would point to the Freemasons. However a close look shows the hand holding the hammer in the center which was the unique insignia of the OUAM. The badge's purpose is unknown, but probably was made for a Fourth of July celebration because of the flags displayed.
Size: 4"

Past presiding officers of JOUAM councils were entitled, like most fraternal organizations, to a special jewel. This example is distinguished by the crossed gavels over the suspension bar confirming the past rank of the wearer. The "ribbon" is not made of cloth but rather is enameled and silvered metal. The name "John Brown" is crudely engraved on the reverse.

restrictions regarding ancestry were removed. The organization's regalia was very closely patterned upon Masonic forms with the result being that there was, and still is, much confusion on the topic.

JOUAM regalia incorporates the Masonic square and compass but without the central letter "G." Instead, in the center of the crossed tools there is an arm holding a hammer. This hand and hammer was in the 19th century a symbol of works and protectionism.

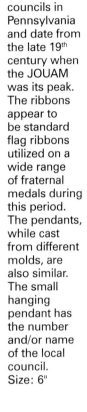

These membership badges are for various councils in Pennsylvania and date from the late 19th century when the JOUAM was its peak. The ribbons appear to be standard flag ribbons utilized on a wide range of fraternal medals during this period. The pendants, while cast from different molds, are also similar. The small hanging pendant has the number and/or name of the local council. Size: 6"

The members' medals are almost always suspended from American flag ribbons (probably the same ribbon stock used for Grand Army of the Republic medals).

XII

The Elks

The Benevolent and Protective Order of Elks, shortened simply to BPOE or "the Elks," is one of the largest social-fraternal groups remaining in the United States today. Founded in 1868 in New York as a social club, the BPOE evolved over time into a fraternal, philanthropic, and benevolent organization. Elk lodges exist in most American towns with some large cities having more than one lodge to accommodate the members. Their halls are identifiable by the large elk head (usually in metal) on the outside of the hall.

The regalia of the Elks features, as would be expected, the head of a multi-pronged Elk stag. In addition, there is a clock face set at 11 p.m., which commemorates the moment of remembrance during public, or private ceremonies, for deceased members.

The Improved and Benevolent Protective Order of Elks (IBPOE) was founded in 1897 in Cincinnati Ohio as a response to the whites-only BPOE. The IBPOE's ritual and regalia are closely patterned on the BPOE. The IBPOE remains the smaller of the two bodies and has an interesting history of involvement with the Civil Rights movement going back into the 1930s.

This member's badge from the Fraternal Order of Elks, while not heavy, is among the largest members' badges made or worn by any fraternal order. It shows a many-pointed stag, clock with dial set to 11:00, and the suspension part with BPOE (Benevolent Protective Order of Elks). The large badge hangs from an equally massive long straight pin. Silvered base metal, probably early 20th century.
Size: 9"

XIII

Knights of the Maccabees

Founded in 1878 in London, Ontario, Canada, the Knights of the Maccabees, shortened to simply the Maccabees, are an insurance and benevolent society with a strong Knights Templar and Knights of Pythias flavor. The Maccabees confer three degrees: Protection, Friendship, and Loyalty.

In 1893, they opened a new headquarters in Port Huron, Michigan, that resembled a Middle Eastern Mosque. That building soon was so widely identified with the Maccabees that they incorporated its exterior onto member badges. Members met in "Tents."

This small member's badge was made of thin metal (probably silver with a gold wash) and enamel. It incorporates the tent that was the symbol of the Knights of Maccabees encampment. Most Maccabees jewels and regalia tend to be small and were intended for wear on the coat lapel rather than as full medals. Size: 2"

XIV

Patrons of Husbandry / The Grange

The Patrons of Husbandry, better known as the Grange, is arguably the most influential rural fraternal organization in America. Founded in 1867 along the lines of a farmer's guild or trade society, the Grange expanded rapidly during the late 19th century. The Grange's membership base was in rural America where farmers found friendship and support in the organization. The Patrons were organized around local affiliates known simply as Subordinate Granges.

This is a set of working tools used as part of the basic ceremonies of a Grange. The tools of husbandry include a plow, axe, etc., and are married with the five-pointed star. This set in base metal and wood was probably the bottom line of what a local Grange could purchase. The author has seen several sets of coin silver tools that were obviously made for more affluent Granges.

This small badge is for a past Chaplain of a subordinate Grange. The role of Chaplain in many organizations is held for a long period of time with the result that when service concludes, the service is honored with a pin. Marked on the back "A. Plaistad/1976-1988."
Size: 2"

There were district, state, and national Grange levels of affiliation with corresponding officers and regalia.

Grange halls were, and still are in many cases, the center of social and civic life in small towns. The two and three story buildings are frequently found on main streets with the first floor today being turned into a general store and the upper levels as apartments.

The Grange, while modeled on Masonic ritual, is unusual in that it admits both men and women. Its ritual focuses upon agrarian life, and the working tools in a Grange ceremony include the plow, spade, hoe, and other implements. Every Grange hall had a miniature set of tools that it used within its ceremonies. The earliest examples of these tools were often made of coin silver although examples in base metals and wood are also found.

Interestingly, Grange regalia tends to be small and not particularly elaborate, although there are exceptions to this rule. Most Grange past officer pins are small and feature the sheaf of wheat badge of the organization.

XV

Knights of Pythias

The Knights of Pythias were founded in 1869 by Justus Rathbone in Washington, D.C. Today, it numbers some 2,000 lodges In the United States and Canada according to their web site. The Knights have the unique distinction of being the first

This image depicts a drill unit of the Knights of Pythias. A quick look would suggest that these are Masonic Knights Templars although a closer look with a glass reveals the shield with the Knights of Pythias shield on the crossbelt. The keystone badge on their chests is probably a member's medal and shows that this team is from Pennsylvania. Circa 1910.
Size 30" x 16"

If you compare this image to that of one of the Masonic Knights Templars, it shows the amazing similarity in the regalia of the two bodies. With the exception of the badges and added fringe, the subject could easily be mistaken for a Knights Templar. He wears a silk ribbon commemorating a meeting held in Pottsville, Pennsylvania, where this image was taken. Marked "Lamont and Mack/Pottsville" and dating 1891-1901.
Size: 5" x 8"

fraternal society to receive a Congressional charter. Why the Knights were first is unknown, but may have to do with the strong anti-fraternal feeling in the country leading up to the Civil War.

The Knights are modeled on the traditional Templar-oriented fraternal groups with a strong crusader and military flavor to their rituals and regalia. Their badge consists of a distinctive blue, yellow, and red triangle with the letters *F, C, B* representing Friendship, Charity, and Benevolence.

This image is difficult to say with certainty that it is a Knight of Pythias, although the shield on the chapeau appears to be of standard Pythian style. Note as well the three metal hangers for the sword. Taken by Bonebrake in Terre Haute Indiana circa 1880-90. Size: 5" x 8"

XVI

The Royal Arcanum

The Royal Arcanum has often been described as neither Royal nor Arcane but rather it was, and still remains, one of the oldest and most successful fraternal insurance and benefit societies in existence. Popular in rural America during the 19th century, the order was an offshoot of the John Upchurch's Ancient Order of United Workmen. Founded by John A. Cummings and Darius Wilson in Boston in 1876-77, it continues today as strictly a benefit society.

This is the pendant jewel of the Royal Acanum's honor degree. Made of brass in Attleboro Massachusetts it would have been worn as a neck pendant. Size: 3"

XVII

Royal Antediluvian Order of Buffalos

The Royal Antediluvian Order of Buffalos, shorted to simply "the Buffs," has been often termed as the "Poor Man's Freemasons." Founded in 1822 in England, the organization began as a drinking society, but evolved by the 1860s into a larger fraternal organization.

The Buffalos is an exclusively English organization with strong ritualistic and regalia ties to the Freemasons. Their officers wear elaborate aprons and have corresponding collars. While not found in this country, Buff regalia has been imported extensively for resale to the collectors' market.

This apron of the Royal Antediluvian Order of Buffalos is a tour de force of design. Based upon a Masonic apron of the period, this example goes one step further with elaborate bullion wire decoration, fringe, etc. While the Buffalos often described themselves as the Poor Man's Masons, their regalia was anything but simple or low cost. This example is English and probably dates from circa 1950. Size: 24"

XVIII

Independent Order of Foresters

The Independent Order of Foresters was founded in England in 1834. The American branch split from the English Order in 1874 and has been primarily focused upon insurance benefits. It is today exclusively an insurance and benefit society. The emblem of the English and American branches is a stag.

This small lapel stud was given to new members of the American branch of the Order of the Foresters. Size: ½"

This badge is probably an English Order of Forester's member badge. Made of thinly struck metal, it has a partial London maker's mark on the reverse. The stag is the most commonly seen symbol of the Foresters and appears on the regalia worn on both sides of the Atlantic.
Size: 5"

XIX

Ancient Order of United Workmen

The Ancient Order of United Workmen was founded in 1868 by John Upchurch in Meadville, Crawford County, Pennsylvania as an insurance benefit society. Its rituals and insignia were loosely patterned on a meshing of Masonic and guild traditions. The badge encompasses the all-seeing eye, square, compass, and anchor.

Pound for pound, this probably is one of the heaviest medals produced for fraternal wear. It is a member's badge for the Grand Lodge of the order. The initials on top signify Charity, Hope, and Protection which were the cornerstones of the three degrees of the Order. The anchor with shield on the badge is the most commonly seen badge of the organization. Probably late 19th century, unmarked. Size: 6"

XX

Knights of the Golden Eagles

The Knights of the Golden Eagles was founded in 1873 in Baltimore, Maryland, as a fraternal society whose ritual and regalia was closely derived from the Masonic Knights Templar. The insignia features swords, banners, crowns, and the conjoined letters *KGE*. It exists to the present, albeit greatly diminished, in the mid-Atlantic.

The central element for regalia of the Knights of the Golden Eagles is the figure of the angel crowning a knight. This appears, along with the cross and crown, as the most common emblems of the order. This is a past President's jewel with the crossed gavels behind the cross and crown motif. Probably early 20th century. Size: 6"

XXI

Improved Order of Redmen

The Redmen is among the most curious and interesting of the nativist/patriotic societies to spring up in the 19th century. Its history is complex and difficult to trace, but members believe that it is the sole contemporary descendant from the Sons of Liberty and the early Tammany Societies who used Iroquois Indian disguises to hide their patriotic work. The organization exists today, although like most other fraternal groups, it reached a membership peak in the late 19th century.

The regalia of the Redmen is highly collected because of its native American associations although most, if not all, was made by non-Indians. Members dressed in costumes loosely patterned on Great Plains and Iroquoian patterns. Most was purchased from regalia supply houses or made by members and thus takes great liberties with traditional Native American clothing. The insignia consists of Indian items including tomahawks, clubs, and war bonnets.

The member's badge of the Redmen includes numerous American Indian motifs including an ax, war club, and bonnet. Redman ritual regalia is loosely based upon stylized American Indian clothing from the Great Plains. This badge would have been worn by members and was probably presented at the time of initiation.
Size: 4"

XXII

Klu Klux Klan

Many books have been written about the White Knights of the Klu Klux Klan and their various incarnations. Historians have divided out Klan history, and its accompanying regalia, into several periods. The earliest materials dating from the post-Civil War period up to the early 20th century and are very rare. Materials from the 1920-40 period are the most common of the three eras and mirror the Klan's broad-based popularity in this period, particularly in rural America. While seeking widespread acceptance in this period, the Klan in the 1930s was particularly violent in the Midwest. Finally, the third period spans the post-war period to the present. This was also among the most violent of the Klan history, particularly in the deep south during the 1960s and 1970s.

Klan regalia begins with the robe and hood worn by all Klansman. The robe is then embellished with the "blood tear" (a red drop of blood) and letters "KKK." Because there is no universal Klan authority, individual state or local factions have adopted their own regalia. In some areas of the country, the white robe of the Klan is not worn as often as a stylized military uniform. All of this is compounded by the fantasy market for

This image is identified on the back as Uncle Lucas Jackson of Athens, Georgia, and probably dates from the 1920s. The subject is wearing the full regalia of a Klansman of the period including hood with removable face mask, robe with double patches, and a red-corded belt. The patches have the cross, diamond, and "blood drop" that were standard regalia of the Klan.
Size: 5" x 7"

The subject is wearing the Klan cross in shield patch while leading a horse for a robed Klan rider. Note the young snooper whose face can be seen peering over the boards on the left side of the image.
Size: 3" x 4"

Klan items produced for collectors and "wanna be" members. Finally, interconnections with the neo-Nazi movement have resulted in a fusion of Nazi and Klan emblems adding one more layer to the puzzle. The short answer for collectors of this material is to study

This striking image shows a mounted Klansman accompanied by a man carrying a Winchester rifle. The Klan in the 1920s and 1930s, despite its overt "peaceful overtones," had a strong violet character as typified by this image. Note the removable face mask.
Size: 3" x 4"

primary sources closely and be constantly suspicious of every item offered.

An interesting side story concerning the Klan in the 1920s-30s was when the organization was trying to become respectable. In Pennsylvania, the Klan undertook the social projects of opening an orphanage in Harrisburg known as Klan Haven. The school offered housing and resources for orphaned children (ironically even suggesting at one point that it would be open to children of all races). The facility lasted a short time until the project failed and the building was sold. Ironically, it is now owned and used by a drug and alcohol rehabilitation clinic.

In the 1920s, the Klan in many states attempted to offer a façade of normalcy for its members and activities. One of the many "mainstream" activities that they undertook was the operation of a children's home or orphanage. Klan Haven in Pennsylvania was originally located in a private home in uptown Harrisburg before moving to a more rural area. This small celluloid pin was produced as a fundraiser by the women of the Klan to support Klan Haven. The bell was to be rung to show your support for the project.
Size: 4"

In the 1970s, one of the many Klan groups claiming originality to the original body was the United Klans of America. Note how this imagery on this window sticker differs greatly from the traditional KKK imagery.
Size: 3" square

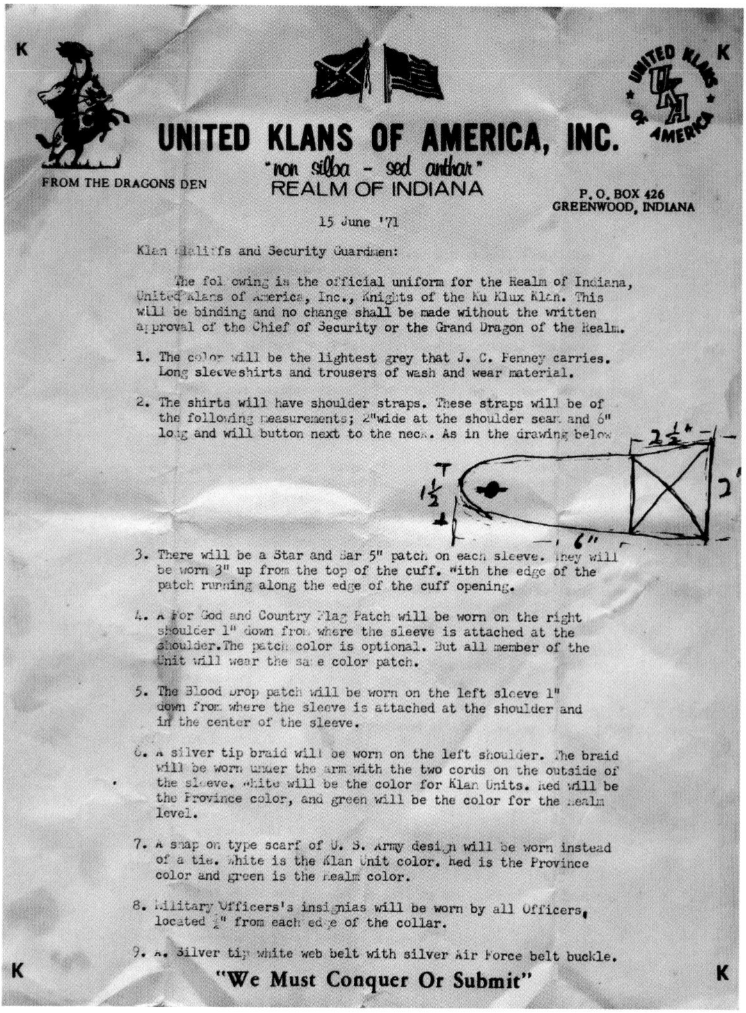

K K

UNITED KLANS OF AMERICA, INC.

"non silba - sed anthar"

FROM THE DRAGONS DEN

REALM OF INDIANA

P. O. BOX 426
GREENWOOD, INDIANA

15 June '71

Klan Bailiffs and Security Guardsmen:

The following is the official uniform for the Realm of Indiana, United Klans of America, Inc., Knights of the Ku Klux Klan. This will be binding and no change shall be made without the written approval of the Chief of Security or the Grand Dragon of the Realm.

1. The color will be the lightest grey that J. C. Penney carries. Long sleeve shirts and trousers of wash and wear material.

2. The shirts will have shoulder straps. These straps will be of the following measurements; 2"wide at the shoulder seam and 6" long and will button next to the neck. As in the drawing below

3. There will be a Star and Bar 5" patch on each sleeve. They will be worn 3" up from the top of the cuff. With the edge of the patch running along the edge of the cuff opening.

4. A For God and Country Flag Patch will be worn on the right shoulder 1" down from where the sleeve is attached at the shoulder.The patch color is optional. But all member of the Unit will wear the same color patch.

5. The Blood Drop patch will be worn on the left sleeve 1" down from where the sleeve is attached at the shoulder and in the center of the sleeve.

6. A silver tip braid will be worn on the left shoulder. The braid will be worn under the arm with the two cords on the outside of the sleeve. White will be the color for Klan Units. Red will be the Province color, and green will be the color for the Realm level.

7. A snap on type scarf of U. S. Army design will be worn instead of a tie. White is the Klan Unit color. Red is the Province color and green is the Realm color.

8. Military Officers's insignias will be worn by all Officers, located 1/2" from each edge of the collar.

9. A. Silver tip white web belt with silver Air Force belt buckle.

K "We Must Conquer Or Submit" K

This broadside was issued by the Indiana affiliate of the United Klans of America in June of 1971. It clearly outlines the regalia worn by the Klan. Note that the Indiana Klan did not wear the white robe in this broadside but rather a paramilitary outfit more in keeping with police or military uniforms.
Size: 8 ½" x 11"

XXIII

The Grundsau Lodge and Fersammling

Although not a national fraternal order, the Groundhog Lodges in Pennsylvania are an interesting sidebar. Founded in 1933 in Allentown Pennsylvania, the Groundhog Lodges were, and still are primarily focused upon keeping the Pennsylvania German language alive. Pennsylvania Dutch (a corruption of the word *Deutsch*) is a unique language derived from 18th and 17th century German dialects with changes added from English over the last 200 years.

Groundhog lodges meet close to February 2nd to determine how much more winter will last. However, they also often meet during the rest of the year at Fersammling/Versammling, which is a celebration in the Pennsylvania Dutch dialect complete with unique foods (often joked as being made of every part of the pig except the squeal).

Each year, many of the groundhog lodges produce a specific commemorative item. This small turtle ashtray is one such example of a commemorative.
Size: 4"

Simply cast by local foundries, the majority of these groundhog lodge souvenirs are neither complex nor highly detailed. Many, like this example, have no purpose except to sit on a desk and remind the member of the particular banquet in a particular year.
Size: 3"

This heavy cast piece was made for Lodge 11 and probably dates from the early 1970s.
Size: 5"

Dated 1991 and from Lodge 8, this unusual stylized figure of a man in a baseball cap is unknown as to its purpose.
Size: 3"

The wheel is symbolic of both nostalgia and also a symbol of finality. This example is dated 1987.
Size: 4"

XXIV

The Orioles

Not to be confused with the baseball team, the Orioles are a 19th century fraternal and benevolent society with strong ties to South Central Pennsylvania. Their insignia is based naturally on the bird of the same name and the local affiliates are known as a "nest."

Naturally the badge of the Fraternal Order of Orioles would have as its central motif the image of an orange and black oriole. This Past President's jewel was given to Herman R. Wager, Past President of Lebanon Nest 147 and probably dates from the 1940s. The pendant, which appears to be a stock item, was made by Robbins and Company of Attleboro, Massachusetts. Size: 5"

D.D.G.P.

This neck jewel is for a Former Master of the Fourth or Patriotic degree of the Knights of Columbus. The regalia of this degree is among the most elaborate of all the Knights regalia. Today, this jewel is worn on the breast along with four or five other jewels showing the progress of the individual in becoming Master.
Size: 18"

The presiding officer of a local council is the Grand Knight. Because of the Knight's history connecting themselves with Admiral Christopher Columbus, the badge of the Past Grand Knight is that of a ship's anchor. The jewel hangs from a purple ribbon with a small Knights of Columbus member badge attached to it.
Size: 4 ½"

XXV

Knights of Columbus

Historical prohibitions by both the Catholic Church and various Masonic authorities has meant that membership in Freemasonry by practicing Catholics has been forbidden. However, Catholic men have long been interested in joining together in fraternal lodges. During the 19th century, many men joined ethnic lodges that often had the tacit support of the local priest. Much of this changed in 1881 when Father Michael J. McGivney and several men gathered together in New Haven, Connecticut, to establish a fraternal society with insurance benefits for Roman Catholic men. Named for Christopher Columbus, the Order has a strong martial flavor to it with swords, ritual uniforms, and elaborate medals being made for wear by the members.

The local affiliate for the body is the Council presided over by the Grand Knight and is usually tied to particular parish. The Council confers three degrees upon its members with a fourth degree, founded around patriotism as an honor degree. The Fourth degree has its own governance and is presided over by a Faithful Navigator. Service in this office allows one to be called a "Former Master."